HITTING HEADLINES

A practical guide to the media

THE AUTHORS

Stephen White is Director of Information for The British Psychological Society. He previously worked in the Publicity Department at NALGO, and has been involved in media training for the last 20 years.

Peter Evans has presented *Science Now* on BBC Radio 4 for over 15 years, as well as making innumerable science, medicine and technology programmes for radio and TV.

Chris Mihill is the medical and health correspondent for the *Guardian*, and previously worked on *Today*.

Maryon Tysoe is a social psychologist, journalist and author specializing in psychology. She writes a monthly column for *New Woman*, and was formerly a staff writer on *New Society* and editor of their 'Findings' page. She has been a regular contributor to the BBC Radio 4 series *All in the Mind*.

HITTING THE HEADLINES

A practical guide to the media

STEPHEN WHITE
PETER EVANS
CHRIS MIHILL
MARYON TYSOE

BPS
BOOKS

Published by The British Psychological Society

First published in 1993 by BPS Books (The British Psychological Society),
St Andrews House, 48 Princess Road East, Leicester LE1 7DR, UK.

Distributed by Plymbridge Distributors Ltd, Plymbridge House, Estover
Road, Estover, Plymouth PL6 7PZ, UK.

A catalogue record for this book is available from the British Library.

ISBN 1 85433 107 8

Typeset by Fakenham Photosetting Limited, Fakenham, Norfolk.
Printed in Great Britain by Redwood Books.

Contents

Foreword   vii

1. WHAT IS THE MEDIA?   1
The press   1
The electronic media   4

2. NEWSPAPERS   7
Getting your story into the papers   7
How is a newspaper structured?   9
What is news? Where does it come from?   16
What makes science into news?   17
Surefire news?   20
Where does news come from?   21
Exclusive stories: are they worth giving?   26
When to contact the press with your story   28
How to write a news story   31
Features: a chance to write   34

3. MAGAZINES   39
Why consider magazines?   39
Magazine staff   40
Feature articles   41
Getting magazines to write about you   42
Writing for magazines yourself   44

4. RADIO & TV   53
Radio or TV? Which do you approach?   53
Getting to know the media to which you wish to
    contribute   54
What's on radio?   54
What's on television?   56
The editorial process: how items get broadcast   60
Different types of contribution   61
Local radio and television: local slant   64
Concepts and conceits   65

Things people worry about   67

5. MEDIA RELEASES   72
What will attract media attention?   74
The four components of a successful media release   75
Design   75
Distribution   78
Timing   81
Composition   83

6. THE MEDIA INTERVIEW   89
The new rules   90
Speaking to newspapers   91
Speaking to magazines   99
Interviews on radio and television   103
Disembodied voices: the 'line' interview   105
Everyday language: forget the grammar book and the
    jargon   107
Questions, questions   108
Visible means of support   109
Practise!   111

Appendix 1: Running a Media Training Course   113
Appendix 2: Being Interviewed – Hints and Tips   129
Appendix 3: Useful Publications   133
Appendix 4: Complaints   134

Foreword

There is more hostility to science than most scientists would care to admit. More and more often there are claims that science, and scientists, are responsible for many of society's current problems; science is responsible for nuclear weapons, industrial pollution, the degradation of spiritual values, materialism, and for the new dangers that genetic engineering brings. Unreasonable as these claims are, we have to recognize that they are widely held.

The only way to deal with such attitudes is by constantly correcting mistaken and false views and putting the case for science as clearly and forcefully as possible. But here there is a problem: scientists have a dreadful reputation as communicators. Whenever I complain about the presentation of science by the media, a constant retort is that scientists are hopeless at communicating their ideas. They can neither speak nor write well, and worse still, are quite incapable of making their ideas accessible to the general public.

Traditionally scientists were not interested in explaining their work to a wider public. There was even the view – perhaps it still persists – that attempting to popularize one's work via the media was not a 'proper' activity for a scientist; that to do so could even damage one's prospects for advancement. This has changed dramatically over the last few years to such an extent that contributing to the public understanding of science now enhances one's reputation. Much of this change in ethos comes from the establishment of COPUS (Committee on the Public Understanding of Science) which is a joint venture between the Royal Society, the British Association for the Advancement of Science, and the Royal Institution. The activities of COPUS are strongly supported by industry and the Research Councils, and for good reason. They all recognize it as essential for scientists to be able to communicate, in as clear and exciting a manner as possible, the nature of their work. Public understanding depends on this communication, and they have a right to expect it.

Communicating science is not just restricted to giving information about a special piece of work. There are two major areas which need particular airing – the process of scientific research and the social implications of science.

Most non-scientists have a very confused conception of the nature of science. (My own view is that science involves an unnatural mode of thought.) The public has very little conception of the variety of styles in scientific research, and, for example, how 'social' science actually is, being both co-operative and competitive. How scientists work, the role of imagination, creativity and very hard work, all need to be communicated. If science is to be integrated properly into our culture, we have to learn to communicate.

The social implications of science present the most difficult problem, however. As scientists we have additional social obligations over and above our responsibility as citizens. Because we understand complex science, which most other people do not have access to, our obligation is to make any social implications of our work public. It is not for us to decide how science should be applied – that is for as wide a debate as possible – and the current discussion of the use of gene therapy provides a good example. Dealing with the media in such sensitive areas requires particular skill.

Public communication of our work is now essential for all scientists, whether we are researchers, applied scientists, social scientists, technologists, engineers or medics. Hitherto we have not been trained in this area, so we should gratefully welcome a text like this which aims to help us redress our deficiencies. Dealing with the media *can* be rewarding; we need all the help we can get.

Professor Lewis Wolpert CBE FRS
University College and Middlesex Hospital Medical School
Member of COPUS (Committee on the Public Understanding of Science)

1 WHAT IS THE MEDIA?

The press □ *The electronic media*

To call the media 'the media' is as inexact as describing all scientists as 'scientists'. Scientists know about their own particular speciality, plus perhaps a couple of closely allied areas. For instance, the astrophysicist is unlikely to understand the latest detail from the quantum theory practitioners while the developmental psychologist would struggle for a complete understanding of the clinical neuro speciality.

The differences between all the sectors and sections of the media are equally diverse, so that even within the main areas like newspapers or radio, the difference between the individual component parts is so great as to make real comparison irrelevant. Therefore, when it comes to working with the media, it is unsurprising that scientists are less than clear about how that general descriptor 'the media' is made up.

As a collective term 'the media' is unhelpful, because each of the individual parts is very different; each works to its own agenda and style and when confronted or contacted by these individual parts our reaction or proaction needs to be tailored to that specific market.

This chapter will attempt to decipher 'the media' by taking a look at the individual parts which go towards making it up.

The Press

Newspapers

Perhaps two things should be said at the outset about newspapers. First, newspapers exist to make a profit. The great majority of their income accrues from advertising, so a newspaper is really a series of stories designed to ensure that the adverts look good. Second, in world terms the UK population buys and reads more national newspapers than anywhere else. But even within this sector of the media the differences are wide; from the *Sun* and the *Sport* at the mass, tabloid end of the market, through *Today* and the *Daily Mail* in the middle, to *The Independent, Times* and *Financial Times* at the quality, broadsheet end. They all have market niches, they all have identified readerships, they all have political (generally with a small 'p', despite common mythology) stances and they all have agendas. *Chapter 2* gives more detail on how these agendas are set and by whom, but as an illustration, in February 1992, the *Daily Express* started a feature series on the psychology of relationships. This topic was then quickly covered by its direct rivals – the *Daily Mail* and *Today*.

So agendas are not necessarily pre-set as long-term strategies by the upper echelons of senior editors. In fact, more often than not, they are set by what their rivals do (for example, *The Sunday Times'* serialization of Andrew Morton's book on the Princess of Wales), or by other extraneous and external factors.

As scientists we may all 'know' about the national press but there are many types of newspaper which go towards making up the whole. There are many regional daily papers, and most areas have an evening daily paper. Add to this the weekly 'paid for' and 'free' titles and the picture is nearly complete. But, of course, there are also the specialist weekly newspapers like the *Times Higher Educational Supplement* or *Angler's Mail* which bridge the strange gap between 'newspaper' and 'magazine'. They want to be seen as newspapers because that brings with it the cachet of immediacy and topicality, but they also carry a large proportion of 'features' material more commonly found in the specialist magazines.

The national Sunday papers also form a category of their own. Whilst they carry some news, more of their pages are devoted to 'comment' and 'opinion'. The object of this (at least in the qualities) is to provide the buyer with a product which can last all week. And as someone who spends a great deal of time on Intercity trains, this object seems to be successful. I often see various *Sunday Times* or *Observer* supplements being devoured on the Tuesday or Wednesday of the following week.

Magazines

Magazines, although described as a 'sector' of the media, very nearly defy description. Think of just about any subject and there is a magazine for it; think of almost any human (or inhuman) activity and you'll probably find a magazine devoted to it. (*Bluebell News* is actually about the railway of that name; *The Strike Gazette* has got nothing to do with tenpin bowling; *Best Advice* is a publication in the insurance sector; and *Singer Big Nine Plus* is listed under 'hobbies'.) At present there are just over 7000 magazine titles in print in the UK. Each year a couple of hundred close and a couple of hundred new ones pop up, attempting to find a market niche or directly competing with an existing title or titles.

Generally magazines don't aim at topicality in the same way as newspapers do, although they all carry news. However, this will be news which is so specific to their audience that they know that no one else will carry it, or news that the editor believes is a 'must' for his or her readers. Usually magazines carry 'features' which are an extended form of storytelling and/or explanation.

Within the gargantuan magazine sector there are majority sections, such as 'women's magazines' like *Woman's Own*, *Woman*, and *She*, which sell vast numbers of copies of each issue. Then there is the 'general interest' sector, including *Good Housekeeping*, *Company*, *Ideal Home*, *Cosmopolitan*, which tends to be the very glossy monthlies. One then moves into the specific interest market, which at present seems to be dominated by computer magazines, followed closely by anything to do with motors and motoring, followed by the leisure and hobby areas. Science comes a long way down the list, both in terms of number of publications and in terms of circulation.

Freelance journalists and the press agencies

The freelance journalist. These individuals (there are thousands of them) are used increasingly within all sectors of the media to provide news and features to order. They usually work in fairly narrow areas, for example, science, or for identifiable sectors of the media, such as women's magazines. Freelancers work in two ways: either they are commissioned by a news or feature editor to write on a given subject, in a given way, and to a given length; or they generate the ideas themselves and then try to sell that idea or story to the news or feature editor. This latter method is preferred by the freelancer and this is why they can be useful to us in getting our story ideas out into the media world. If you can cultivate a freelance journalist or three, then you cut down the distance between you and the various editors. In fact, they can almost act as a kind of agent on your behalf. Also, because they only make money by selling their ideas (and words), they can be a very useful source of advice as to the 'saleability' of your story.

Press agencies. These are organizations, independent of individual media titles, who make their money by selling news and features to individual papers, radio and TV stations. Most agencies do not receive commission. They work by writing what they want to and hoping that someone will buy it, although some of the smaller geographically based agencies will be commissioned by newspapers to cover, say, local football league games or local courts.

The largest purely UK-based agency is the Press Association (PA). This has many specialist correspondents (although not a science one) as well as lots of generalists and feature writers. All their material is sent out 'on the wires' to both national, regional and local media outlets. These individual papers or radio stations pay PA for the totality of their service. They pay to have the wire from PA's Fleet Street base, and then use whatever they want, either as straight copy or as source material.

PA also has a reporter, more usually known as a 'stringer', in just about every town in the country. So making contact with your local press agency or local PA stringer can mean your story and your research being seen and read all over this country and possibly abroad.

Although accessing the different sectors of the media print industry is basically the same in terms of how to get your story into the system (but more of that later in *Chapter 2* on newspapers) the same cannot be said of radio or TV – the electronic media.

The Electronic Media

Neither radio nor TV is homogeneous. They are no more than a compilation of different programmes with different objectives, often targeted at potentially quite different audiences. One could argue that the different parts of a newspaper – news, features, editorial, letters, city, sport, reviews – are analogous to a day's or a week's output from a radio or TV station, but from the listener's or viewer's perspective the experience is very different. A newspaper can be 'owned' and read *in toto*, whereas radio and TV can never be 'owned', unless you were to spend the whole of your life tuned in so that you could experience the whole range of output. This just isn't possible, and research shows that we are much more discerning about our listening and viewing than we are about our reading of newspapers.

Radio and TV are split between the BBC output and that of the independents. But even within this split there are an enormous number of different output mechanisms.

Radio

BBC radio now has five national channels plus the World Service, as well as a plethora of local stations based in towns and their hinterlands, and regional/national stations in Scotland, Northern Ireland and Wales. All this output, which can range from obscure opera on Radio 3 to Welsh language talk shows, from the latest rap music to science magazine programmes, is supposedly tailored to 'the audience'. This audience has been market researched and is constantly monitored by viewer and listener panels, and programmes are continually evaluated on the basis of their position in the audience figure charts. As in every part of the communications industry, little is left to chance and everything is planned with the objective of building, holding and expanding the audience.

Independent radio is another ball game. A network of stations now covers the whole of the UK and the characteristic feature of the great majority of them is pop music. These stations are unashamedly attempting to reach a younger audience, but as competition in this sector has grown they are also attempting to cater for very specific interest groups amongst their potential audience. For instance, several of the coastal stations run programmes for the boating fraternity as well as giving very detailed shipping forecasts; in cities such as Bradford and Leicester where there are large immigrant populations, individual programmes are targeted in a very specific way.

The local radio station can be likened to a local newspaper. To be of interest to the station, the news has to be local, with the abundance of independent radio phone-ins akin to the 'Letters' page in the local paper. Of course it must be recognized and remembered that these stations earn their income from advertising.

Television

TV at the latter end of the 20th century is a rapidly changing and developing beast. Soon there will be five channels in the UK and this together with satellite and cable will make up a daunting array of media opportunities. However, TV, and to a lesser extent radio, is undergoing another revolution and that is in the commissioning of independent producers to make programmes. This was begun by Channel 4 and is now happening more and more in the BBC and within the ITV network companies. Whereas in the old days it was relatively easy to find the right person in the BBC to talk to, now you might have to chase round a multitude of independent companies to find out who is doing what and when.

News output is still unaffected by this development, but it has already reached current affairs, and logically there is no reason why *Horizon*, *Antenna*, *Tomorrow's World* or *Panorama* should not be under the control of an independent production company within the foreseeable future. Although this is not necessarily a detrimental step, it is one that we need to understand if we are to effectively use and communicate with particular programmes, outlets, stations and channels.

• • •

The rest of this book will look in detail at these different media sectors and explain not only how they operate, but how we can access the various parts, and how we can and should react when they contact us.

2 NEWSPAPERS

Getting into the papers □ How is a newspaper structured? □ What is news?
□ What makes science into news? □ Surefire news? □ Where does news come
from? □ Exclusives □ When to contact the press □ Writing a news story
□ Features

Getting Your Story into the Papers

Newspapers are not *per se* interested in science, or psychology, or academic research, or even in medical advances. What they are interested in are news stories, and news stories which affect people. The difference is not one of semantics. An awareness of what newspapers, and indeed the whole of the media, want, and how they operate on a day-to-day basis, is crucial to understanding why some areas of science are reported while other areas, arguably more important, are not.

Scientific hearts will no doubt immediately sink, and researchers fear they will have to play to the gallery and 'prostitute' their learning if they want the transitory pleasure of a few column inches of publicity.

'Playing to the gallery' is a deliberately pejorative phrase; but what happens if instead of this contentious phrase we substitute 'making our work accessible to the public'? How many scientists would hold this to be an ignoble or unworthy aim? Hopefully not too many. In a society which appears increasingly ignorant of the value of science and indeed may be frankly hostile towards science, it would seem to be time for scientists to stand up for themselves and communicate clearly and effectively about what they are doing, and why.

Apart from the altruistic desire to educate the public, publicizing your work can have important practical benefits in a world of soft money and short-term research grants. The most worthy alpha-rated project can have funding turned down, but even the most cash-strapped of grant-making bodies shies away from creating banner headlines along the lines of 'Pioneering Research Unit To Close'.

Accepting that scientists do want people to know what they are doing, whether from an altruistic desire to educate or a need to raise funds, how do you then get your story into the newspapers?

Science or medical stories have no automatic right to a place in a national newspaper, or even to sympathetic or special consideration. Outside of national newspapers, which might be expected to consider the wider public good, regional or local newspapers have even less space or appetite for general science. However, the 'local angle' – which we'll return to later (p. 36) – can be an advantage. In general, science stories have to compete on their merits against all the other news of the day: politics, economic news, foreign stories, crime, education, consumer affairs, social services, defence, the Courts, and, on popular papers, the Royal Family, showbiz and a mass of 'people' or 'human interest' stories.

Some stories are 'sexier' than others. The expression rarely has to do with sex itself but is newspaper-speak for stories that are seen by journalists to be intrinsically interesting and likely to appeal to a wide audience. A new drug which can help children with cancer, even though it is a rare cancer, is likely to rate more space than a paper in *Nature* on plate tectonics even though the latter might be deemed to add more to our general scientific understanding of the world.

The 'So what?' test

Every story, wherever it originates, has to pass the 'So what?' test. Science stories, more than most, are cursed by the 'So what?' factor because they are less immediately understandable than a murder, political row or pop star's divorce. The 'So what?' test is exactly what it sounds. A reporter will bring a potential story to his or her boss, the news editor (or other senior journalist on the news desk), succinctly sketch out the details and be bluntly informed 'So what?'

This question means a host of things to professional journalists. Who does the story affect? How many people's lives will be touched by it? Will it change anything? Will anyone be interested or moved or outraged by the story? Does it say something about our society or the way we live our lives now? Is it whacky enough, different enough, to make people smile or discuss it in the pub, even if it isn't of earth-shattering importance? So what? One of the more important skills of journalism, which no one ever teaches at journalism school, and which the public, quite understandably, has no idea about, is overcoming the 'So what?' factor. In short, a good deal of journalism is about selling the story to the news desk.

How is a Newspaper Structured?

In theory at least, the news desk is the hub of newspaper operations. The news editor is very important, almost more so than the editor, in the working lives of most journalists, who very rarely get to speak to the editor or have their presence acknowledged by him or her. The news editor, or one of his or her two or three deputies, accepts or rejects a story on the spot, usually while speaking to someone else on the phone or looking at news agency copy on a computer screen.

There's no court of appeal unless reporters want to push their luck very hard and go over the news editor's head to one of the deputy or assistant editors or even to the editor. This is an extremely high risk strategy because an editor is unlikely to back a reporter over the news editor. If they do, news editors are not going to be happy and have a great many means at their disposal to exact revenge. These can range from refusing to run subsequent stories, assigning the reporter unpleasant or tedious jobs, putting the person on weekend and night duties, docking expenses, arguing against pay rises and even nominating the person for dismissal on the grounds of incompetence. Hiring and firing can rest absolutely with the news editor and certainly with the editor, and sackings on the spot are not unknown.

Part of the reason some journalists are driven to unprofessional activities is the sheer fear of losing their jobs if they don't get the story. A public shouting match with the news desk is not a pleasant experience, nor is the threat of the sack. Rather than a reporter trying to go above the news editor, a more plausible scenario is for the reporter to rephrase the précis of the story, pleading that he or she had not expressed him or herself clearly, and desperately adding additional elements, in the hope that 'Mark II' will find greater favour. It rarely does.

Foot soldiers and specialists

Reporters are the foot soldiers of newspapers, generalists who are talented at asking questions, but usually without specialist knowledge in any particular field. They are usually told what stories to

cover by the news desk, and rarely, at least on national newspapers, do they bring in their own stories.

Specialists, the correspondents such as the education correspondent, the crime correspondent and the medical correspondent, are
a much more privileged breed. Because they have their own
specialized area, they are largely left alone by the news desk on the
understanding that they will generate their own stories. They are
expected to be aware of everything that is going on in their patch
and be *au fait* with all the important personnel in that field. This is
no small expectation, but, by and large, it is met.

A medical correspondent, for example, would be expected to
know experts in the areas of heart disease, cancer, paediatrics,
AIDS, mental illness, obstetrics and gynaecology, surgery, old age,
psychology, health economics, medical politics, undergraduate
training, molecular biology and genetic engineering, drug addiction, suicide, radiology, physiotherapy, epidemiology, nutrition,
stress, NHS management, and the patient self-help groups for
every disease which has a name. It's quite possible, in one day, to
write about how plastic surgeons re-attached a policeman's arm
severed by a sword-wielding drug addict; how commuters at a
major rail station will cope with post-traumatic shock following an
IRA bomb blast; and the reaction of trade unions to health authority plans to axe 500 jobs at a large teaching hospital.

Other journalists

In addition to reporters and specialists, major newspapers have a
battery of political correspondents, headed by a political editor
who invariably feuds with the news editor over the space given to
a Commons debate about tax reforms versus the space to be given
to a report into the causes of a major plane crash.

The Financial or City staff have their own fiefdom and also fight
with the news desk about whether the value of the pound against
the deutschmark is a better story than a sex abuse scandal in a
boys' home.

The Foreign Desk staff, with the help of a few staff correspondents and news agencies across the world, have the whole planet
as their patch. They are always arguing with the news desk over
whether a flood in Pakistan or a massacre in Croatia is worth more
space than a corrupt police inspector or a survey into the TV viewing habits of the average Briton.

The Sports Department is a self-contained empire, but occasionally breaks out from its back page ghetto onto the news pages if a household-name athlete is suspended for taking steroids or a top club is fined for football hooliganism.

The Features Department is an entire operation complete unto itself, supposedly co-existing with news but more than usually ploughing its own separate and sometimes contradictory furrow. Features are longer news analyses or comment pieces – 'behind the scenes' explanations, 'a patient speaks out about her horror operation' type articles, or 'why can't the police catch the killers?' polemics from retired experts. (See pp. 34–36 on features.) Some features are written by the paper's own specialists, and some are commissioned from outside experts such as academics or politicians. Most are usually written by full-time feature writers, who are generalists rather than specialists.

Leader writers

A unique and self-contained element of newspapers are the leader writers. These are anonymous pundits who set out the paper's prescription for curing the ills of the nation in their reserved section of newsprint (usually alongside the Letters). Sometimes the editor will personally pen these if it's something he or she feels strongly about. Usually, however, they are composed by professional leader writers, although they must first clear their ideas with the editor. They are a team of senior journalists who see themselves as the intellectual High Table of the paper and are seldom bothered by the fact that few people actually read their words.

Named experts, economic commentators or academics, are also invited to fill the centre of the paper with their thoughts on the current crisis on the day, as are the in-house bylined columnists, usually the senior political or economic staff. The leader columns and the analysis pieces may go largely unread but since they are written by the editor and his or her lieutenants, they are always held to be deeply important to the appeal of the paper.

Sub-editors: the word technicians

Apart from the reporters and specialists, the people who do the real work on newspapers are the sub-editors (the subs). These are an unsung army of word technicians who take the copy from the reporters, specialists and news agencies and shape and cut and hone, and sometimes mangle, the words into the space allocated for them on the page.

A reporter may have written a 600-word story but the editor may have decided it is only worth 200. If there is time, and the reporter is still around, they may be asked to cut it themselves. But it is more likely that the subs will do it, especially as much subbing is done at night when the reporters have disappeared.

Most subs are highly-skilled former reporters who can condense a piece without losing its sense, and in some cases thoroughly improve it with a little judicious pruning. Others are less skilled and end up distorting things, although perhaps not intentionally. It has to be said that some distortions occur because the reporters or specialists write sloppy, confusing copy to begin with.

On the tabloids, although not on the qualities, most subs hold most reporters in the highest contempt and would sooner die than show them the subbed version of the copy. Such rivalry does no one, least of all the reader, any good, but it is very common. There is a saying in newspapers that the strongest urge known to a human being is not sex or greed, but the urge to tamper with another person's copy!

Crafting the headlines

It is the sub-editors, and not the reporters, who write the headlines. Many people labour under the idea that the journalist whose name appears on the story writes the headline. This is not true. Headline writing is an art and few reporters ever see the headline or are asked for their opinion on it before it lands on their doormat the next day.

It is a highly skilled job to sum up a story in two or three words, and if the largest typeface is being used, this is all there is room for. Trying for wit or humour with only a handful of short words makes crossword puzzles look easy. Ideally the headline should tell you in a glance what the story is, or else intrigue you enough so you want to find out what it is by reading on. Sometimes scientists complain that the body of a story is basically correct, but the headline is sensationalized. Sometimes it is. But if it has persuaded people to read the story, it has worked.

The news list – the news conference

Two vital elements in setting the agenda of newspapers are the morning and evening news conferences.

The morning news conference. The news desk and the heads of the other departments will have compiled a list of the stories they know are coming up that day or issues that deserve coverage. Around 11 a.m. there will be a conference to talk these through, decide on the priorities, and, very roughly, start allocating space to each of the stories. Pictures, graphics, accompanying editorials or a feature reflecting the background to that day's big report will all be decided upon at this conference.

Reporters live in trepidation of bright ideas emerging from desk-bound executives anxious to impress the editor at the morning conference. The 'find Martin Bormann' syndrome has ruined many a reporter's day. If there's a report on the failure of the organ donor card scheme, for instance, it's quite probable that some hotshot, who, of course, won't have to do it, will suggest finding the country's longest surviving transplant patient. This may, or may not, help to illustrate the issues, but it will certainly mean a day of unrelenting ringing round for the luckless reporter or specialist deputed to do it. The fact that the person, when tracked down, doesn't want to talk will be seen as the reporter having screwed up a great conference idea.

Despite anxieties about the executives 'improving' the story with their great ideas, it helps if something is on the morning list, and discussed at conference, because everyone in authority then knows about it and is mentally counting on it to fill a certain slot. The decision-makers know, however, that what sounds good in the morning may turn out to be a damp squib by the afternoon. The opposite is also true; something which looked unpromising can turn out to be far more interesting later in the day.

The unknown and unpredictable have to be allowed for – the proverbial plane crash – so morning stories are not locked in concrete, but they are expected. The editor is updated with promising stories throughout the day, and at 5 p.m, or thereabouts, the second major conference is held to plan the next day's paper in detail.

The evening news conference. Decisions are now made about what is going on the front page and what the main stories on the other pages will be, and how long they should be. At this stage, stories are beginning to become more locked into the production process, although major news which breaks later can be accommodated.

However, as it gets later and later, it gets more and more difficult to persuade the desk that an interesting but previously unmentioned story is worth something – that is why the earlier something is written, the better. Getting your stories on the morning or evening news list, and having them discussed at conference, is no guarantee they will go into the paper, but it does give them a major advantage.

Newspapers print more than one edition, so it is possible for stories to be changed or updated as the night wears on. This can sometimes result in people in Scotland and Cornwall, who get the first editions, reading different stories to those seen in the London edition, which is printed last.

Getting a quart into a pint pot

Scientists, whatever their field, all moan from time to time that not enough newspaper space is devoted to their work. Perhaps this is true. But, if it is any consolation, every other profession and section of society feels the same way, from one-parent families to opera buffs. The reason is not wilfulness or a disregard for the value of science, but a question of space. Every day newspapers juggle to fit, not just a quart, but usually a gallon, into a pint pot.

As an exercise, count the number of news stories per page on the Home news pages of whatever national or regional paper you read. (Home news are UK as opposed to foreign stories.) On the broadsheet papers, the *Guardian*, *Independent*, *Times* and *Telegraph*, the average is usually five, allowing for pictures and 'nibs' – the 'news in brief' paragraphs often run together down the edge of a page. On pages taken up with large adverts, the number of stories, again with pictures or graphics, may be three. Even on completely 'open' pages, pages with no adverts whatsoever, there are rarely more than seven stories.

On the tabloid papers such as the *Mail*, *Today* and the *Express* the average number of stories per page is three. In some cases, where there is a very strong human interest piece with good pictures, it may be just two or even one.

The 'pops', the *Sun*, *Mirror* and *Star*, run many one- or two-paragraph stories, but more substantial pieces usually number two per page or sometimes just one.

A handful of stories to say it all

Excluding the front pages, which can be dominated by a mix of Home, Foreign, City or Politics, the number of Home news pages in the broadsheets is around five or six. This is a moveable feast depending on whether there are big or small papers that day, which in turn is determined by the number of adverts people want to place. If there are only a small number of pages, even the most important stories get squeezed, and the peripheral ones will be dropped altogether.

Home news can also be affected by international events of great significance, such as the Gulf War or the fall of Communism in Russia. UK stories will be curtailed to allow more space for such overseas events. Major political or financial events such as the resignation of Ministers or the collapse of the pound can also lead to traditional Home news pages being hijacked.

Normally, however, on the broadsheet papers there might be five Home news pages, with perhaps five stories on each. This means that the whole of life, across every section of society throughout the UK over the preceding 24 hours, has to be represented by just 25 stories. Under such constraints of space it could be argued that far from getting a bad 'show' it is a wonder that science does not get a worse one.

Simplified – or cut to size?

Scientists and other researchers are quick to say that when their stories do appear they are frequently trivialized or oversimplified. If this does occur, it is not because of malice or incompetence on the part of the journalist, who probably fought very hard to get the piece in the paper in the first place. Again, it is to do with space – the tyranny of the column inch.

As a follow-up exercise to counting the number of stories, count the number of paragraphs within each story. On the broadsheet papers, a page's main story ('page lead' in newspaper-speak) will usually have between 15 and 20 paragraphs. Subsidiary stories may contain 8 to 12. The main stories in the *Daily Mail* and its sister papers consist of 12 to 18 paragraphs on average. Page leads in the *Mirror* or *Sun* may be 8 paragraphs.

Each paragraph is roughly 30 words. A page lead on the *Guardian* may therefore be around 600 words, on the *Mail* 360, and the *Mirror* 240. The luxuries of space and time, which academics and researchers enjoy when a paper is prepared for a peer review journal, simply do not exist for daily paper journalists. Stories have to be written in hours, and sometimes within 10 or 20 minutes if a deadline is looming. The absolute essentials are crammed in, with a few quotes for flavour, maybe a paragraph or two of reactions from people affected by the findings, and that is it.

What is News? Where Does It Come From?

Deciding what's newsworthy

Why do journalists choose to write the stories they do in preference to others? How do reporters, and their superiors, judge that one piece of information is newsworthy, while another, delivered at the same time by the same person at the same meeting, is not? There's no hard and fast answer, no rule book, no objective set of criteria, no news 'micrometer' that can be applied to each event to see whether it passes or fails the news test. It is an intangible decision-making process, largely based on experience and intuition; arbitrary, almost whimsical.

Some journalists have a far better 'news antenna' than others. A throwaway remark, a chance aside, and suddenly their eyes light up, 'ahh, that's interesting. I didn't know that', they think to themselves. The process is almost palpable and there's a kind of mutual telepathy over an item's newsworthiness amongst experienced journalists. This occurs especially between those who work together regularly, such as the specialist correspondents from rival media outlets who may see each other at different jobs three or four times a week. The idea that reporters and specialists out in the field are in deadly competition with each other is largely a myth in terms of day-to-day working. However, the exclusives, the 'scoop' that only one paper has, or being first to report the contents of a major report, are all highly prized and are not shared. But at press conferences or scientific meetings it's fairly normal to see journalists in a huddle at the end, checking that they have taken the quotes accurately. They are also asking each other 'What's the line? What's the intro?' In other words, what is the most important point that emerged and what will be the first 30 words of the story?

Same meeting, different lines

Journalists frequently take different lines from the same meeting, depending on the seriousness or popularity of their market and sometimes the political complexion of the paper. From a meeting on the epidemiology of cancer, for instance, it's possible that the *Guardian* would highlight the different incidence rates between socio-economic groups. *Today*, because of its strong anti-smoking policy, might focus on the rising toll of lung cancer amongst younger people, while the *Daily Mail* would possibly be more interested in statistics on breast and cervical cancer, to appeal to its female audience. The *Mirror* might want to reflect on the North–South divide in cancer rates, while the *Sun* might pick up on the potential value of antioxidant vitamins as a protection against cancer, probably with a headline along the lines of 'An orange a day keeps the tumour at bay.'

By and large, however, there is a remarkable consensus between the various papers as to what is news. If something is news, then the same story, albeit longer or shorter, is likely to appear in all of them, just as it will on TV and radio.

What Makes Science into News?

It helps if something:

- is genuinely original;
- is being said for the first time;
- will affect thousands of people;
- is worrying;
- is controversial, different or amusing.

But it is a highly subjective business; the bottom line is that a story is a story if a reporter thinks it is. The fact that something was 'said yesterday' at a scientific meeting or conference can make it new as far as journalists are concerned, even though the work in question might be familiar to the discipline. Publication in a journal makes it new, even though the field work might have been carried out years ago.

On the other hand, yet another report saying that cholesterol is bad for the heart and smoking bad for the lungs, even though a new group of patients has been studied, is not going to excite anyone. Apart from 'So what?', the glummest words a news editor can say to a journalist are: 'We know that, don't we?'

Therefore, stories can become news because of the 'Gee whiz, I never knew that' factor. Put more crudely, some news editors talk about the 'CFM factor' – they read a story and say 'Cor! F*** me!' Stories with CFM appeal usually get into the paper. Other stories make it because of the style and presentation rather than the contents. Some do so because of the status of the presenter or the status of the subject being scrutinized or criticized.

Make it interesting

'Gee whiz' stories might be dismissed as the stuff every school child should know, but doesn't. This includes facts such as how fast a dinosaur could run; how many stars are visible at night; what percentage of the human body is comprised of water. Basic, but still interesting. So too is the wonder of science, which sometimes scientists themselves forget. Just how do cells know to turn themselves into organs rather than skin? Why is it that the immune system of a mother doesn't reject the baby? How is it possible for the human mind to conceive of ordering words or musical notes or brush strokes in such a way that it can leave others profoundly moved?

The 'How does it do that?' piece, even though some of the answers are simply not known, can sometimes make very good copy.

Sexy soundbites

Sometimes the way things are presented can make them news, even though the contents might not be startlingly original. A nice 'sound bite,' as they say on radio, or a 'sexy' quote, can often mean the difference between something 'making' – getting in the paper – and being 'spiked' – not used.

For instance, it's hardly news that many young children smoke. But large headlines resulted from one British Medical Association press conference because a media-aware doctor deliberately said that shopkeepers who sold cigarettes to children were as bad as heroin pushers in the death and misery they caused. This may, or may not, have been an exaggeration, but it allowed a presentation of the issues about underage smoking which would otherwise have been dismissed by news editors as old hat.

On another occasion a dry-as-dust session at the annual conference of the British Association for the Advancement of Science was saved from oblivion by a happy thought from the speaker. The technology of devising metals that could retain their shape when warm was all very well, but the 'So what?' factor was looming large. Then, 'It could be used to make a bra that would remember the exact shape of the woman', said the speaker. That story appeared in virtually every national newspaper, allowing far more coverage of the detailed science of metallurgy than would normally be the case, because of that one single line.

Use analogies and metaphors

Analogies, metaphors, frames of reference that ordinary people can understand, can mean the difference between a largely unread scientific report and a newspaper article which will be seen by hundreds of thousands, or even millions, of readers. It is an uphill struggle to get these aids to understanding from many scientists. The fact that every person consumes so many kilos of sugar a year in their average diet means nothing to most readers. But when a professor of dentistry says 'The average person eats a pile of sugar the size of a cricket ball each month', that gets headlines.

Use real life

Using real-life examples or real-life people, even though their identities are not revealed, can ensure science gets into newspapers where normally it would be written off as too specialized. (See pp. 34–36 on features.) It cannot be stressed often enough that newspapers, and other media outlets, are not scientific journals and they are not platforms for scientists to address their peers. The rules are different. Not sloppier, not less rigorous – just different.

A debate on whether Asperger's Syndrome is a separate disorder or a subclass of autism may fascinate psychologists, but it does nothing for the public. That debate *did*, however, receive considerable coverage because journalists probed for real-life examples of how Asperger's manifests itself and the researcher was happy to supply them.

People with this syndrome obsessively collect carrots; the light fittings of British Rail carriages; the colours of the doors of magistrates' courts, or anything else it is possible to collect. The fact that these people were not simply eccentric, a kind of 'super trainspotter', but suffering from a form of mental condition was intriguing. The real-life details of their habits brought the story alive. These weren't laboratory subjects, they were people.

In terms of making news the applied does have the edge over

basic research, because it's rather more obvious what it is for. All this means, however, is that basic scientists have to try that little bit harder to be media aware.

What possible interest can the morning train commuter be expected to have in sequencing the genome of the nematode? On the other hand, 'Humble Earthworm Unlocks the Secrets of Life' is a damn good read.

Status does count

Sometimes the status or notoriety of a person makes a story news where similar offerings from someone else would not. Complaints by junior doctors that they are still expected to work horrendous hours would not get much of a show, but a similar complaint by the President of the Royal College of Surgeons would be a different matter, especially if he was prepared to say patients' lives were being put at risk.

Rightly or wrongly some personalities are more newsworthy than others. Journalists flocked to cover speeches by Edwina Currie, however mundane the subject, because there was a chance she would say something controversial. Lectures by Hans Eysenck or Lewis Wolpert are far more likely to generate media interest than those by other equally eminent scientists, because they have a track record for being controversial.

Attacks on the Government are far more likely to produce press coverage than an anodyne report which simply says more money is needed, or, even more tamely and all too usually, more research is needed. The right-wing Adam Smith Institute calling for more privatization is not news, nor is the Labour Party calling for re-nationalization. If the two swapped positions, *that* would be news.

Surefire News?

There are some ingredients which ought to guarantee a place in any newspaper, but nothing is certain. The Princess of Wales getting AIDS or the Pope eloping would seem surefire bets; however, a decision to scrap income tax or the announcement of war could knock even these off the front page. One utterly compelling headline, used by an American supermarket magazine, came pretty close to being the ultimate science story. It read: 'New hope for the dead'.

Bentham versus the one-off

In deciding why one story gets coverage and another doesn't, a very rough rule of thumb is the Benthamite principle that the issue which affects the most people is probably going to be more newsworthy than that which affects a few. However, there are frequent and wholesale exceptions, particularly concerning individual tales of courage or fortitude. There are many 'miracle baby operation' or 'pluckiest girl alive' stories solely concerned with individuals. As a general rule, though, cancer and heart disease usually rate more coverage than rare genetic conditions. But, if the condition is rare enough, such as children who have to live inside oxygen bubbles to protect them from infection, this becomes newsworthy simply because it is different.

A petition from a host of eminent scientists supporting the use of animals in experiments may not be news, despite the eminence of the signatories, on the grounds that 'They would say that, wouldn't they?' But a single letter published in *Nature* from an unknown Jamaican opthalmologist saying that ganja and white rum can help fishermen see at night is seen as news because it is so unusual.

Richard Peto, the distinguished Oxford statistician, has complained on more than one occasion that journalists prefer the novel to the worthy. But this is the very nature of journalism. If scientists want to get their message across they have to do more than restate old news, however worthy.

Where Does News Come From?

Mail

Despite the popular myth of the dedicated newshound sniffing out buried exclusives after months of relentless sleuthing and secret meetings with unnamed sources at midnight rendezvous, the prosaic truth is that an awful lot of news comes by post.

The pile of mail on the desk of specialist correspondents each morning is usually six inches high and on some occasions, especially if they've been away for a few days, feet high. Much of it is junk mail and hits the bin in seconds: invites for new ward openings in Cleethorpes; a charity appeal by the Brighton Rotary Club; the financial results of an American chemical company; a puff for a new book about aromatherapy. Others may include the offer of an off the record briefing at 4 p.m. with an expert on hayfever. None are of any use to busy national paper journalists.

Useless PR firms – useless news

Sometimes scientific bodies employ the services of expensive commercial public relations companies to put their message across. With a handful of exceptions, they are seldom worth what they charge.

Drug companies are among the worst offenders for calling useless press conferences, but other scientific bodies are also guilty. What is the point in withholding the speeches and the background information until after the people have spoken, or inviting you to interview the chairman before you've heard what he has to say? Both are commonplace. Huge press packs are produced about drugs or other products of marginal interest for diseases with which journalists are already familiar, while press conferences are organized at times in the afternoon which would make it almost impossible to get the copy into the next day's paper even if one were interested. The inverse law of press conferences is that the more lavish the location, the more vacuous will be the contents.

The only point in holding a press conference, which some scientific bodies as well as drug companies have still failed to grasp, is if you have something to say and are prepared to say it. The publication of an annual report that doesn't say anything, the establishment of a new department which isn't going to be doing anything special, or the setting up of a fund-raising appeal for something that already exists elsewhere, is not a reason to hold a press conference.

There are a few first-class PR firms, especially those which work only with noncommercial medical or scientific bodies. But the best press material is generally prepared by in-house press officers from charities or learned societies. The Imperial Cancer Research Fund, the British Heart Foundation, The British Psychological Society and the British Medical Association all have first-rate press operations which many other scientific and medical bodies would be well advised to study.

Universities and hospitals, especially Trust hospitals who want to publicize themselves, are waking up to the value of efficient press liaison. But most continue to bumble on, content with a phone call out of the blue stating: 'The Professor is sure you'll be interested in this'.

Journals make news, sometimes

Academic journals provide another rich source of stories, and the more clued-up amongst these, such as *Nature, The Lancet* and the *British Medical Journal*, have recently taken to issuing their own press releases in advance of publication alerting journalists to what they consider the most newsworthy stories. Journalists receive the journals 24 hours in advance of the publication date, on the understanding that they do not publish until that day, to allow them to prepare their stories. This embargo understanding, which applies to most press releases, is a useful convention, and one which is honoured in 99% of cases, because it helps both the journalists and the organization concerned. (See *Chapter 5* on media releases.)

Scientists, perhaps rightly, dismiss journalists as generalists, but in terms of breadth of scientific reading most specialist correspondents probably see far more periodicals than many scientists. A typical weekly consumption for a medical correspondent would consist of: *The Lancet,* the *British Medical Journal,* the *New England Journal of Medicine,* possibly the *Journal of the American Medical Association, Nature* and *Science* if there is no science correspondent, *New Scientist, Doctor, Pulse, General Practitioner,* the *Pharmaceutical Journal, Nursing Standard* and *Nursing Times.* If the paper has no social service correspondent, then *Community Care, Health Services Journal* and others all have to be added. In addition, there are a plethora of monthly magazines which may yield stories. These include the *Journal of the Royal Society of Medicine, The Psychologist,* the *British Journal of Addiction* and the *Journal of the Royal College of General Practitioners.*

The Government news machine

The Government ministries, quite apart from parliamentary activity, are a constant source of news. The Department of Health and the Department of Education, for instance, will issue three, four or more press releases each day. Opposition parties, the trades unions, and affected professional or patient groups often issue their own press releases in response to these.

Government department news offerings do have to be taken with a very large pinch of salt, however. The Government's news management is a black art which can reduce even experienced journalists to tears of frustration. Favourable statistics are issued promptly and preceded by a phone call from press officers to alert journalists to the fact they are coming. Unfavourable announcements, such as a rise in prescription charges, an increase in hospital waiting lists, the freezing of child benefits, cuts in allocations to the Research Councils, are sneaked out at 6 or 7 p.m. or even later at night. They are also issued on Friday afternoons; just as the House of Commons is about to rise for annual holidays; or at big set piece events when attention will be elsewhere, such as Budget Day.

The Press Association

Another major supplier of news is the Press Association, known universally amongst journalists as PA. This is the national UK news agency, similar to Reuters abroad or Associated Press, the major American wire service. Apart from its own staff reporters and specialists, PA is fed by a host of local reporters ('stringers') up and down the country. These are either freelance journalists, or reporters employed by local or regional papers supplementing their incomes with a bit of unofficial freelance work. In addition, most large towns have their own small news agencies who, apart from selling directly to newspapers and other media, often file to PA as well.

The PA service is comprehensive (although less so in recent times because of staff cuts) and straightforward, but is often confined to the main points of the story rather than background explanations or interesting details. Generally it is better at set piece news events such as train crashes or court cases than expositions of scientific advances.

The blessing, and the curse, of PA is that it sets the news agenda for every major news organization. This is true for Fleet Street papers, Radio Four, *News at Ten*, the BBC's *Nine O'Clock News*, as well as for all the regional morning and evening papers, and the regional TV and radio. If something is on the early morning PA news schedule, news editors expect it to be covered and will include it on their own news lists. A meeting on occupational psychology in Glasgow, that from the agenda might not have looked all that interesting to the specialist, suddenly becomes much more newsworthy because the desk will have seen that it is on the PA list.

If there's a piece on PA about a scientific paper in *Nature*, the news editor will immediately come over and ask the science editor if he or she is going to write about it, and if not, why not. This, from the in-house specialist's point of view, is the curse of PA. If PA has the story, everyone else will have it, so the story gets written to ensure that the paper is not scooped by rivals. This can mean lesser stories taking precedence over more important ones.

PA staff, like all other journalists, are human. They have off days, make mistakes, catch the wrong end of the stick or suffer misplaced enthusiasms. Therefore, if an inexperienced PA reporter believes a potentially helpful, but experimental, cancer drug is a 'Wonder Breakthrough Miracle Cure' this can get on the wires. News desks will then start jumping up and down and clearing space off the front page and demanding pictures and graphics and interviews with boffins and real stories from patients who have been helped. The in-house specialist then has to spend an anxious and often acrimonious half an hour explaining the real details of the story, why it is not a wonder breakthrough miracle cure, and why the paper, while it should run the story, should not put it on the front page as this would only raise false hopes.

It only takes one mistake in a piece of PA copy, or misplaced understanding, for the mistake to appear in scores of newspapers. Nevertheless, any scientist who wants publicity should always ensure that PA knows about the event or report, because their interest will ensure wide coverage.

Other sources of news

Other sources of news include readers' letters, 'follow ups', personal contacts and other media. Readers do frequently write or telephone, wanting to complain about some local issue or other. Often their letters would be better directed to their local newspaper, but sometimes they contain the elements of a national story.

Similarly, scientists, particularly if they are protesting about closures or under-funding, can sometimes find themselves in the news columns rather than on the Letters page.

Follow up stories are what they sound like – going back to a previous story to see what happened. Did that researcher ever get any results on that study he was starting which we wrote about last year? How is that patient on the new therapy progressing? All that fuss about inadequate facilities, how was that eventually resolved?

After a while on the job most journalists build up their own contacts in various fields; for instance, professors of oncology, the directors of MRC research units, transplant specialists. The occasional phone call and general query of 'anything interesting going on?' can sometimes produce stories that would not otherwise be in the public domain.

The media as a whole is extremely incestuous, and rival outfits apart from PA can set the news agenda with the stories they are carrying. Radio Four's *Today* programme, for instance, is often still news 24 hours after it was broadcast if it carried a controversial interview with a government minister. What appears on the *5.45 p.m.* and *Six O'Clock* TV news, as well as the flagship TV news programmes at 9 p.m. and 10 p.m. can strongly influence newspapers. A story by a staff member which had been relegated to the bottom of the news list as unimportant, and potentially droppable, may receive renewed interest because the TV people thought it was important.

Exclusive Stories: Are They Worth Giving?

A great deal of looking over the shoulder goes on within the media to see what the rivals are up to, so getting a story in one outlet is often a very good lever to get it into others. This raises the tricky question of planting exclusives – the giving of a story solely to one news outlet. Although newspapers and the other news organizations pay great lip-service to the importance of exclusives, from the scientist's point of view in trying to place them there are a number of real disincentives in doing so.

It may sound perverse, but the fact that a newspaper has a story to itself may make it *less* likely, not more, to give it prominence. Theoretically, having the story to oneself affords time to properly research it, talk it over with the news desk and thereby ensure it is given a lot of space, preferably on the front page, so that rivals will gnash their teeth when they see it and be forced to follow it up, albeit 24 hours late. In practice, however, the news desk might well say: 'If we've got it to ourselves, let's hold it for a dull day when there's not much else happening'. The story then hangs around in the news queue getting dustier and dustier until the news desk no longer believes it is news because they've been looking at it for so long. Another reaction, not unknown, is for the desk to say: 'If no one else has got it, it can't be much of a story'.

One of the best ways to get a story into the *Guardian*, or any other paper, is to say: '*The Independent/Times/Telegraph* are all on to this – we can't afford to hold it.' This plays on the rivalry factor.

Forcing the pace

Journalists are experts at putting things off until tomorrow, if they have the luxury of time, in order to deal with the urgent stories of the day, or to concentrate on administrative matters, or take someone out to lunch. An exclusive which needs a lot of checking, even though the anonymous brown paper envelope contained an intriguing report, can tend to get pushed further and further ahead. If, however, the envelope also contains a note saying 'Have also sent to other papers' the reporter is immediately galvanized into action to escape the wrath of the desk if a rival runs it first.

From the scientist's point of view, the other risk with exclusives is that other papers may not follow them up. They may accept they have been scooped and not want to give prominence to a rival's glory, or they may feel there is going to be nothing more to say by the next morning, especially if there has been saturation coverage on TV and radio. Journalists also have long memories and are good at carrying grudges, so all those whom you have not made privy to the exclusive are not going to be friendly the next time you want coverage.

Unless the contents of the exclusive are so perfectly tailored to one paper, perhaps because it is likely to give far more sympathetic coverage than others, then by and large placing exclusives can *reduce* rather than increase news coverage. If you've got a good story, give it to as many people as possible.

Sunday papers – a mixed blessing

The same risks apply to giving stories only to the Sunday newspapers. Some PR firms labour under the delusion that giving things exclusively to the Sundays will ensure widespread coverage, with the Monday papers automatically following them up. But despite their vast size, there is sometimes surprisingly little hard news in Sunday papers, with most space being occupied by comment and analysis in the heavies and human interest stories in the pops.

Although they have more time to prepare their material, Sunday paper journalists generally only get one story in a week, if that. If they fail to sell their science story to the desk, they've missed the boat for another seven days, by which time someone else is likely to have carried it. Moreover, if there is a big, late-breaking news story on Saturday, the proverbial plane crash for instance, the science story may well be dropped with no chance of it being resurrected the following week. If Sunday stories do appear, but are only deemed to be of marginal interest, they may well not be followed up, because daily news desks will feel 'we've seen that – it's been and gone'.

There is also an in-built resistance by daily paper specialists to admit they have been scooped by their Sunday colleagues, some of whom have a reputation for being rather more creative in how they judge the value of a science story. There is a real temptation, when the desk rings the specialist at home on Sunday morning inquiring about yet another so-called exclusive in one of the Sundays, to tell the news editor: a) it's old b) it's rubbish c) the reporter's mad.

If Sunday stories are followed up, especially if they have been heavily hyped, there is a danger for the scientist whose work is featured that the subsequent pieces will turn into knocking copy, when a host of other scientists with opposing views are marshalled to say how flawed the study is. Far from becoming famous, the scientist then finds him or herself pilloried and derided.

When to Contact the Press with Your Story

News stories have an extremely short shelf-life and are far more perishable than eggs or even fish. In general, if they are not used within 24 hours, they are not going to be used. It may sound arbitrary that a report two years in the making which fails to be covered when published in *The Lancet* on Friday is not deemed still newsworthy on Saturday or Monday, but that is how it is. Sometimes it is possible to resurrect a science news story for use as a feature or on one of the science and health pages now run by most newspapers (see p. 17). Stories can sometimes be saved if there is a genuine follow up, for instance if the Government or a research body decides to set up an inquiry panel in the light of the report's findings, or a sufferers' group calls for compensation because they've been harmed by the drug or surgical technique. The contents of the original report can then be detailed, but this doesn't often happen.

Avoid busy news days

It is a fact of life in the news industry that some news days are busier than others. This is largely unpredictable, but, with some planning and a little luck, advantage can sometimes be taken of this to ensure coverage which might not otherwise be given. As has been said before, a plane crash, bomb blast or death of the Queen cannot be anticipated and will generally blow any science story out of the paper. But there are some known busy news days, which can be avoided, and quite a few known slack days which can be targeted.

If you have the luxury of time and the ear of a friendly journalist it is well worth asking a good few weeks in advance if anything else big is going to be happening on the day you are planning your press conference or report launch. If there is another major event, it might be worthwhile rescheduling your news conference, either for a different time or a different day.

Sometimes ill luck dogs the most newsworthy of conferences, especially if they have to be organized perhaps years in advance and cannot be changed. The 1992 Annual Conference of The British Psychological Society opened on April 9 – the date of the General Election. Perhaps surprisingly, stories did still appear, possibly because they were seen as an antidote to the wall-to-wall political postmortem. In 1990, the annual meeting of the Family Planning Association coincided with the resignation of Mrs Thatcher. Teenage pregnancies and new contraceptive methods are usually newsworthy, but not against that sort of competition.

There are some fixed points in the news calendar which can be avoided, such as Budget Day, the Autumn Statement, and the Queen's Speech. However, it is still possible to find PR firms organizing press conferences on Budget Day and then wailing the following morning that they didn't get any coverage.

Timing is all

The time of day when a press conference is held can make a big difference to whether or not something is covered. Mid-morning is generally best, between 10.00 a.m. and 11.30 a.m. This will not suit evening papers and may be tight for the *One O'Clock* TV and radio news, but it does ensure that most newspaper journalists will attend and be able to file their stories in good time.

Even on busy news days some of the early pages (those nearer the middle of the paper) have to be prepared as not everything can be left to 7 p.m. Providing a nice little EPL – early page lead – can make a journalist very popular with the desk, and perhaps ensures that the piece gets more coverage than it would if it were written at 6 p.m.

Afternoon press conferences are usually a waste of time, and hacks don't like breakfast meetings because they have to get up early and because these smack of American-style hype. It might not be convenient for your department/section/funding body to hold a press conference at 11 a.m. whereas 4 p.m. would be much easier. But the question you have to ask is – do you want news coverage or not?

Sunday for Monday

Just as there are busy news days there are also slack news days. Usually these cannot be predicted, but there is one slack news day every week which rolls around without fail – Sunday. It comes as a minor revelation to many people to realize that daily newspaper journalists work on Sunday. But this is only common sense – Monday's paper has to be put together by someone. There is never usually much news happening on a Sunday, so it can sometimes be a struggle to fill the pages. Scientists can therefore use the 'Sunday for Monday' embargo system to get coverage that might not otherwise be given.

Reports, studies, policy statements, even new books, can all be sent to papers for use Sunday for Monday. The reporter or specialist will usually be extremely grateful, because desperate news editors start asking on Friday or even Thursday 'Got anything Sunday for Monday?' They do not want to have to go into the morning conference on Sunday with an empty news list.

It pays to send Sunday for Monday stories out a few days early, so that they arrive on Wednesday, Thursday, or Friday at the latest. This will allow them to be written on Friday and left in the news desk queue. If the stuff arrives on a Saturday it is possible, indeed likely, that the specialist or reporter may not physically be around (although they will be on call at home) and the material will lie there unopened until Monday morning when it is too late.

Seasonal slack days

Other classic slack news days are Bank Holidays, and especially the Christmas period. Pieces about injuries to bell ringers, the psychological meaning of Santa Claus, and the physical properties of champagne bubbles, have all appeared as serious (or semi-serious) science stories because there was nothing else around at Christmastime.

Needless to say, August is generally a pretty slack time, although, of late, upheavals in the former Soviet Union and the

Gulf have reversed this trend. Academics themselves tend to be fairly thin on the ground during August, but if there's a report you want published that is interesting but not earth-shattering, August is a good time to release it.

How to Write a News Story

It is unlikely scientists, doctors or psychologists would ever be asked to write a news story for national newspaper, although they might be asked to write a feature. (See p. 34 and *Chapter 3* on magazines.) A little knowledge of how a news story is constructed can help scientists tailor their message to fit this format. Moreover, news writing skills are virtually the same as those needed for writing press releases (see *Chapter 5*) which researchers can often find themselves doing, and the discipline is very good practice for constructing clear but concise internal reports.

A science news story is a précis of the main findings of a study or conference written in a way that is of interest to, and will be understood by, lay people. The first paragraph – the *intro* – must sum up in 30 words or so the newest and most important points of the story in a way that will make people want to continue to read to find out more.

News stories are the complete opposite of learned journal articles. In journals, the background is set out, the methodology painstakingly gone through, the results itemized one by one, and only at the end are conclusions and implications discussed. Virtually without fail, the very last paragraph of a learned journal article can become the first paragraph of a news story. News stories have their own internal chronology which has nothing to do with the way real life events unfolded, or the logical, if stolid, step-by-step approach of a journal report.

The inverted triangle

News stories follow the shape of an inverted triangle. The essential stuff goes in first, and the more detailed, but possibly expendable material, goes at the bottom. If space is tight, subs traditionally cut from the bottom. It doesn't, therefore, pay to put the explosive quote at the bottom even if it does make a very good sign-off line.

That is why, with court cases, for instance, it might seem logical to read exactly what the villain did and what the defence and prosecution barristers said, and then be told what the verdict and jail sentence was. But written this way, the prison term is likely not to appear because the last paragraph will have been chopped if space is short. Instead, the sentence and the judge's comments will come as the intro or at least paragraph two or three, because they are newsworthy and this will minimize the danger of them being inadvertently cut.

Similarly, with science stories, the results and the implications should come first, and only at the end do the details of exactly what was done or the background to the study appear.

The five Ws

Journalism courses traditionally state that the intro should consist of the five Ws – **Who?**; **Why?**; **What?**; **When?**; and **Where?** There are, however, dangers in trying to cram too much into the first paragraph, and generally it's best to set out the most telling point as powerfully and clearly as possible and leave it at that.

The second or third paragraphs should develop and reinforce the main finding. Around paragraph four it's not a bad idea to put in a quote. Reproduce the exact words of the report or scientist, spelling out the implications and the importance of the findings. 'Although still experimental, if the technique is found to work it could be the most exciting development in energy generation since the splitting of the atom', is something readers need to be told early on, not in the final paragraph. At this point in the story, if there is opposition, reaction, or a Government comment, it's best to put it in. The details can be given later, but a sentence along the lines of 'Greenpeace and Friends of The Earth immediately condemned the report as liable to lead to widespread environmental pollution,' tells the reader that there is more than one side, and can make them read to the end to find out what these views are.

Like playing fish, the idea is to draw the reader painlessly through the paragraphs to the end, without introducing sudden indigestible lumps of information which make them flee to the diary column or the sports pages in search of light relief.

Forget the methodology

Scientists are obsessed by methodology, but this can be the kiss of death when trying to hold the reader's attention. Sum it up in one paragraph, if possible. 'Six hundred middle-aged men received the drug and a further 600 the placebo. After a two year follow up twice as many men on the dummy pill had died as those taking the active drug.'

A news story is NOT a journal article. Nobody cares about the significance ratio or the confidence interval unless these are so dubious they call the study into question, in which case it's probably not a news story in the first place. Often scientists will give results and not say what the mechanisms of the action might be. But subs and readers will want to know if the heart drug does work, *how* does it work? Readers don't want a lesson in pharmacology but one line saying the drug is believed to widen blood vessels, thereby easing high blood pressure, will put them out of their misery and fend off the inevitable sub's query about 'How does this work?'

Spell out the implications

It isn't enough just to stick rigidly to the findings if the implications are screaming out for clarification. If men really are deliberately seeking out unsafe sex in an area rife with AIDS, then the researchers who discovered this must attempt to explain why, even if ideas about the risk of death as an added thrill might be seen as speculation in strict scientific terms. 'How will health educators reach this group?' is a valid journalistic question, even though it was not part of the original project. Regardless of what the authors think are the most newsworthy points of their report, the journalist is the judge.

The reaction is also news

If a report is controversial, then reaction from the Government, Ministers or affected groups must be sought by the journalist. Wider questions must be addressed in the news story. It may be feasible to transplant parts of an aborted foetus into the brain to attempt to mitigate the effects of Parkinson's Disease, but is it ethical? If nuclear power really can be linked to leukaemia, what are the Government and the industry going to do about it? This reaction can become the main story, leaving even less space for the original report. This might sound unfair, but that's the nature of the game.

Forget the jargon

Scientific terms should not appear in a news story for a lay audience unless they are clearly explained. It cannot be assumed that readers have ever heard of a monoclonal antibody, let alone know what one is. Most readers will not have a clue about the work of Jean Piaget, so a few words of explanation, even if it is just 'educational psychologist,' are necessary. Even if it means using up precious sentences, or even a paragraph or two, sometimes the scientific background, which is taken as read by the researchers, must be set out, in simple language, or the subsequent development which the report is about will make no sense.

However, there are only 12 or so paragraphs in a news story, so the preceding work must, of necessity, be brutally condensed. It isn't a history lesson, and the news must be emphasized. Although it might be the very last paragraph, a story on a new treatment for breast cancer might state: 'Some 25,000 new cases of breast cancer are reported every year in the UK and around 15,000 women die.' That information will not have been in the report but it helps the reader understand the point of the research.

Features: a Chance to Write

Scientists are far more likely to be asked to write features than news stories. (More about features will be given in *Chapter* 3.) In short, features on newspapers are longer, less time-driven, more personal or more analytical than news stories, but they must still be topical. Topical in newspaper terms means within the next few days after a news event, not next week or next month. The failure of a safety system on a nuclear power station may prompt an in-depth piece, within 48 hours or even for the next day's paper, by a nuclear engineer on why the problem occurred and what measures are built into such plants to ensure that a Chernobyl-type explosion could not happen in the UK.

After disasters, it is not uncommon to have an accompanying piece somewhere in the paper by a psychologist looking at the possible effects of Post-Traumatic Stress Disorder on both victims and rescuers.

Such newspaper features require scientists to write quickly. The time and space constraints are different to those for news stories, but the need to be newsworthy remains paramount.

Another type of feature, particularly in the heavyweight papers, may be an analysis or critique of Government policy, say, with regard to science funding or proposals to close major teaching hospitals in favour of boosting family doctor services. Such articles are expected to be more technical than news stories, but they must still be readable for a lay audience. It is no good throwing in a quick reference to the Pilkington report if you don't remind people what the Pilkington report said.

Sometimes polarized views or polemics are deliberately encouraged, with the hope of sparking off a debate in the Letters column. You can then enjoy the rare luxury of flaunting deeply held prejudices. It is possible such pieces may be contrasted with those of the opposing camp; for instance, for and against animal experiments, for and against nuclear power. Before taking up the cudgels too enthusiastically, it might be worth bearing in mind whether the subsequent public reaction will be enjoyable or difficult. There may be nothing wrong with being 'Professor Nuclear Power' in the public mind, but in these troubled times being 'Professor Vivisection' or 'Dr Abortion-On-Demand' may cause problems.

Real people, real events

An article for a lay paper, even though it is written by a scientist on a scientific subject, must be of general interest. One of the best ways of ensuring this, as with holding press conferences, is to use real people or real events to illustrate the story. In fact, if you propose talking or writing about work that involves people, you will, in most instances, be asked by the person commissioning the feature for real life cases. Scientists, especially doctors or psychologists, are naturally reluctant to expose research subjects, patients or clients to the full glare of media publicity. There are also ethical and professional rules about divulging confidential details without the person's consent. Sometimes in features it is acceptable to use fictionalized patients based on real cases, but this must be made clear in the copy. The piece should start with their problems and only then go into what the profession can do to help, where the research is going, what the implications are for the future. Ideally a good feature will end with the same people it started with, showing how they have been helped.

Interviews. Research subjects are often extraordinarily keen to talk about their experiences. Provided they have not been coerced or forced into doing so, many patients seem to positively enjoy talking about their operation or new drug treatment. Some want their five minutes of instant fame, some want to pass on potentially good news to others, some see it as a way of thanking the doctor or researcher who helped them. If they want to help, let them. Most journalists are not monsters and do not want to ruin people's lives with prying questions. They well understand the nerves that ordinary people feel when asked for an interview. Often these ordinary people will speak with such moving simplicity that it transposes worthy but dull science into headline news.

Easing the psychological scars of disaster victims is all very well as a news story. But when one of the victims of the King's Cross fire, speaking five years after the event, can still say 'at night the demons come', that drives home far more starkly than acres of journal reports just why the research is so important.

Apart from real people, the real events, the true history of how a piece of research was undertaken can bring an article to life. Scientific advances are usually the result of collaborative, painstaking, incremental processes, rather than the 'Eureka!' insight in the bathtub. Sometimes a chance remark or observation, an unexpected overlap with a colleague's work, the thought while out jogging, can mean an important step forward, and these are the things that readers want to hear about because they humanize science.

It isn't shameful to talk about the frustrations and the disappointments, or the excitement or exhilaration. That is what people want to hear. If it was the Friday afternoon 'just for the hell of it' experiment that produced the result rather than the mainstream, directed research programme, then that is a good story. Tell it.

Curiosity and enthusiasm are infectious. If conveyed to readers they can sweep them through an article which originally they would have considered as abstruse or irrelevant. A newspaper science feature is a chat about what you do, to a friend who is reasonably intelligent but unfamiliar with your work. You want your friend to say: 'Hey, you make it sound really interesting!' If that happens, that's good journalism.

The local angle – exploiting geography

Aside from national newspapers, TV and radio stations, there are a host of regional and local newspapers, TV and radio stations. The regional dailies such as the *Yorkshire Post*, the *Manchester Evening News*, and the major Scottish papers, such as *The Scotsman* and *The Herald*, carry international and national news in the way Fleet Street papers do. However, they are also very keen to carry local stories, and this can be exploited.

The regional dailies are fairly parochial. The local weeklies – the much derided 'local rag' – are totally parochial. A plane crash over their circulation border will not interest them unless it knocked off chimney pots in their patch on its way down, or their fire brigade was called to the neighbouring area to give help. One enterprising regional paper even reported the sinking of the *Titanic* as 'local man in boating tragedy'. It's easy to make fun of this parochialism, but it can be a powerful ally in getting science into the public domain if it is properly harnessed.

If you live or work in their area, daily or weekly regional papers are automatically going to be more interested in you than national papers which are swamped with stories from across the country. A researcher from Leicester University may have trouble in persuading the science editor of *The Independent* that his or her research is interesting, but he or she is likely to get a sympathetic hearing from the *Leicester Mercury*.

Many regional daily papers have their own medical correspondents, if not a science correspondent, and it is well worth getting to know these and cultivating them. Often pieces which first appear in local or regional papers are picked up by Fleet Street and run the following day.

Some news agencies make a living by doing little more than retelling local stories to national papers which might not otherwise have known about them. A new operation to cure snoring, using a laser to burn the palate, and devised by doctors at Papworth Hospital, Cambridge, appeared in many Fleet Street papers. It came from a freelance in Cambridge after local publicity. Everyone has a local newspaper, TV or radio station – it makes sense to exploit this geographical advantage.

• • •

To sum up, newspapers are chaotic, time-driven, irrational, frantic places and the appeal of science stories has to be very obvious if they are to win space against so many other competing stories.

- The constant pressure upon the news desk is to say 'So what?' so scientists have to make an even more determined effort than most to explain their work, because sometimes its immediate relevance or importance is not obvious.

- Reporters or specialists do not have absolute control of their copy, and because of the pressures of time and space, sometimes what appears has to be a compromise between what the scientist might ideally like and what the journalist thinks is feasible.

- Scientists can help to ensure that their research makes it into the public domain by using frames of reference, analogies and metaphors which the public can understand. Real-life cases and real-life anecdotes about how the work was done also enliven what can sometimes be seen as worthy, but dull, research.

- Apart from approaching national newspapers directly, an effective route for the wide dissemination of information is the Press Association.

- Regional dailies and even weeklies are more sympathetic to local scientists and their stories in turn often filter through to the national press.

- There are dangers, as well as benefits, in giving stories as exclusives, but there are slack newsdays, especially Sundays, when papers are grateful for science material because there is less happening on other fronts.

3 MAGAZINES

Why consider magazines? □ *Magazine staff* □ *Feature articles* □ *Getting magazines to write about you* □ *Writing for magazines yourself*

Why Consider Magazines?

Magazines offer a vast outlet for scientists' work, research, news and stories. Not only are there specialist science magazines such as *New Scientist*, and quasi-specialist magazines such as *New Statesman & Society* and *The Economist*, but there are huge numbers of general interest and women's magazines which publish a great deal of material on such subjects as children, health, psychology and medicine. The famous weeklies, such as *The Spectator*, have their own idiosyncratic target audiences; there are a small number of glossy magazines for men, such as *GQ* and *Esquire*; trade magazines for every profession and industry; and hordes of specialist magazines in every area of life from management and astronomy to economics, computers and motorbikes. It is also a fluctuating market, as every year new magazines appear and existing titles expire.

Many magazines have extremely sizeable circulations. Some weekly women's magazines clock up over a million; some monthlies around a quarter of a million. Readership (as opposed to those actually buying the magazine) figures are even higher. But circulation figures should not be your only criterion for approaching a magazine – magazines with smaller circulations may have a target audience which you would like to address.

Magazines – with the odd specialist exception – are often not even considered by scientists as vehicles to publicize their work. With such sizeable and/or specially-interested readerships, however, they can offer a highly effective channel into the public arena.

Magazine Staff

Unlike newspapers, magazines usually operate on skeleton staff. If you look at the masthead – the 'cast list' of magazine staff which normally appears near the front of the magazine – this becomes clear. If you do not count the sub-editors and production staff, the art department (responsible for organizing illustrations, photos and so on), the 'contributing editors'/'contributors' (people not on the staff, but who are columnists, regular contributors or consultants), the advertising personnel and lists of personnel in the company which owns the magazine, you are often left with a very small number of staff writers and editors.

Editorial staff

The overall editor stamps his or her mark on the style of the magazine, has to approve all commissioned pieces, and may do a considerable amount of commissioning him or herself. The editor may do some detailed work on accepted pieces, but mostly this would be done by the section editors and the subs. The overall editor also does a lot of management tasks, such as hiring and firing staff and making presentations to advertisers.

The remaining editorial staff may either be writers only, or may write articles themselves *and* be responsible for editing a particular section. In their editorial role, they have to come up with ideas, commission writers to do pieces on those ideas, deal with unsolicited material and the ideas of regular – and hopeful – contributors. The phone lines echo with 'Yes, well, I don't feel that the readership is *quite* ready for an article on that particular kind of sexual abnormality; but, yes, there might be something in the idea of coping with childish tantrums . . .' When the copy arrives, often a lot has to be done to the text to make it 'right' for that particular magazine's audience and style. Section editors have been known to rewrite features completely, cursing. This may be because the information in the piece is interesting, but is, say, presented in thickets of dense prose, or badly structured, or full of suspect grammar, convoluted constructions, or appalling jokes. The section editors often have to think of, research and write pieces of their own too in addition to wading through piles of daily post the height of Canary Wharf and answering a phone which rings every five minutes.

Freelances

Because of the pressures on the in-house staff, it is simply imposs- ible for them to produce a great deal of the material that finally appears themselves. As a result, magazines rely heavily on free- lances. As the name implies, they work for a variety of publi- cations, and are paid article by article. Sometimes they will be given a retainer or placed on contract, thus becoming more locked into a particular publication and producing regular pieces for them. Friendly freelances, as we shall discuss later, can be a boon to scientists.

Feature Articles

Unlike newspapers, magazines are features- rather than news- oriented. Newspapers are expected to hit the wastepaper basket the next day; magazines are kept for days or weeks by readers, who dip into them. Magazines prefer longer, more reflective articles to short items. This is partly because their lead times – the gap between the last piece of copy (written material) arriving and the magazine going to press (being printed) – are longer. For monthlies, the lead time is usually two to three months, and many features are already completed and sub-edited long before that. Even the weeklies' lead time is greater than 24 hours, which makes competing with newspapers, radio and TV for current affairs news stories just a touch difficult. The weeklies can sometimes comment on news stories which have already broken, even if they do not produce them themselves.

However, magazines *can* break the news of recent scientific research if the newspapers have not already done so, and, with their insatiable need to find topics for features, provide scope to discuss a particular area of work at some length. (Magazine features tend to be around 2,000 words; newspaper features are usually at the most around 1,200.) So features are the name of the magazine game, and these offer a lot of potential – and under- exploited – space for science and its applications.

Sampling some of the mainstream magazines over a couple of months revealed articles on:

the psychology of serial killers, 'virtual reality' and ophthalmology (yes, called 'The eyes have it') in *For Him*;
the London Futures and Options Exchange, medical aspects of

caffeine consumption, and chromosomal checks for female athletes in *GQ*;

how anti-oxidants work, Japanese business practices, the technology of interactive TV, and car alarms in *Esquire*;

human 'guinea pigs' in medical research, adultery, and diamond-edged drills as a possible alternative to major coronary bypass operations in *Good Housekeeping*;

prostitution, and cancer survival rates in *Cosmopolitan*;

prisoners' wives, adultery (again), gynaecologists, and the health benefits of pet ownership in *She*;

the psychology of relationship maintenance, stress counselling in the workplace, and effective drugs for cyclical breast pain in *New Woman*;

mediation for neighbours' disputes, and endometriosis in *Woman*;

aircraft safety, and facial non-symmetry in *Woman's Own*;

preventing strokes, and vaccine for feline leukaemia in *Bella*;

the ozone hole, and irritable bowel syndrome in *Me*.

Some of these topics were covered in full features, while others were short articles. Still others were smaller pieces in a particular section of the magazine, such as the health pages. Magazines are like a gigantic maw, constantly ravenous for information and ideas. There is, as you can see from the sample mentioned, a need and desire for scientific stories and source material.

Getting Magazines to Write about You

Given that magazines on the whole operate on skeleton staff, everything has to be made as easy for them as possible.

If your research is relevant to some current event (such as a child abuse case or a catastrophic flood), then as you will have seen, the magazines are not usually the best place to go. In such a case it would be better to ring the most appropriate newspaper immediately, where they may need scientific research for fast follow-ups of the event. (It may in some cases be necessary for you to clear any media work with your institution/funding body.) However, it is possible that you would be in time to catch one of the weeklies, such as *New Scientist*, which has some flexibility as regards last-minute news stories. Ideally, such a magazine would want you to write a short piece yourself, as they operate under such tight schedules. If you do not want to do that, it is still worth ringing up as they might be able to write the piece themselves.

How to inveigle a magazine journalist into writing about your research

If there isn't a great rush, there are several approaches.

The media release. Preferably, send a media release. It is best to send it to a named person (or a job title), as this makes it slightly less likely to go straight in the bin. If you are unsure exactly to whom it should be sent, either check the masthead or ring the magazine and ask. Mail not addressed to any specific person goes into the bin extra fast.

Do not underestimate the sheer number of media releases that magazines receive. I used to be on the staff at the late-lamented *New Society.* Media releases not specifically addressed used to pile up on a table in the office, and every so often some hapless staff writer would have to clear it. He or she would pull up a big black plastic dustbin, heave a sigh and begin. Eyes would rest on each release for about 0.02 of a second, fingers would flicker so fast they would be a blur, and 98% would hit the bin.

So, to lower the scan rate to 0.05 of a second, address your release to somebody. To really slow them down, of course, you need – or the press officer of your university, organization or learned society needs – to write an excellent release (see *Chapter 5*).

Letter writing. An alternative approach to magazines is to write a letter. Do not, however, enclose an academic research paper and expect the editor to make sense of it or translate it into an article suitable for his or her magazine. The technical niceties of your seminal paper in the *Journal of Cerebral Studies* are simply not going to be appreciated or even necessarily understood.

The best plan is to study the magazine of your choice carefully. Then either write to the overall editor of the magazine, or to the editor of a particular section of the magazine which you think your research would fit into. The name of the section editor will often be on the section itself or given on the masthead. If not, ring and ask who it is.

In your letter say that you've done some research which you think might be suited to their magazine/section, describe it in no more than two paragraphs, and ask if any of their journalists would be interested in writing on this topic. If you get a positive response, this is the time to send them any papers you think are reasonably comprehensible and relevant, and arrange times when you are available to be interviewed.

Other approaches. If neither of these approaches – the press release or the letter – works, there is still a chance that the journalist will register your name. Later, if the magazine is looking to write or commission an article in your general area of interest, they may ring you up as part of their research for the piece, or pass your name on to the journalist they commission to write it. So you can sneak your research into the magazine that way.

A last possibility is to make yourself known to the appropriate press officer of your organization or learned society. Let it be known that you are willing to talk to journalists (from magazines or newspapers) about your particular area of expertise. Press officers are usually desperate to know whom to pass journalists on to, and if good science is to get to the public then good scientists are the ones who should be telling them about it.

It may be that after a while you will strike up friendly telephone acquaintanceships with freelance (as well as staff) journalists, who will keep coming back to you for help and quotes for different articles they are writing. This way you can gather a few phone numbers, so that when there is something new and interesting in your research that you would like publicized, *you* can ring *them*. Freelances, like all journalists, constantly need new ideas to write about. Staff journalists at least get monthly salary cheques; for freelances, each idea = one article = eating. So never be afraid to ring them up.

Writing for Magazines Yourself

It may be that you would like to write about your research and area of expertise yourself. The climate of opinion in the British scientific community about contact with the media is slowly changing, and the public understanding of science is becoming a valued aim. Therefore, to write for magazines will provoke far less horror among colleagues than it did in, say, the early 1980s, though perhaps still a little envy . . .

Assuming that you don't have to write the piece in a terrible rush because it's not linked to some hot news story – which you would probably have to be quite confident and experienced to do – then what is the best plan?

Choosing the magazine

The very first move is, of course, to choose your magazine. It may be that you are certain of this – it's obviously the most appropriate for your area or it's your favourite. But if you're not quite sure, don't close your options too quickly. It can be very informative to go into a large newsagent's, and walk slowly past all the shelves. Magazines are grouped according to target audience, and you might get some ideas about whom to approach that you would not have thought of otherwise. If you are a counselling psychologist, you may not have particularly thought about the magazines for nurses; if you're a medical researcher, many magazines have health pages; if you're a computer expert, have you appreciated *quite* how many computing magazines there are? So it's worth a 15-minute walkabout for research purposes. You may also find it helpful to supplement your hands-on prowling (for which there is really no substitute) with a reference book such as the *Writers' & Artists' Yearbook*, which includes pretty comprehensive lists of UK and other English-speaking countries' newspapers and magazines.

Having chosen your magazine, it is absolutely essential to study it carefully. This might sound obvious, but the fact is that many would-be contributors simply do not do so. The journalist Jonathan Sale, writing in *Journalist's Week*, asked editors what they looked for from freelances like him:

> 'The single thought that first occurs,' snapped Peter Fiddick of The Listener, 'applies even to so-called professionals. It is nice to find that somebody has actually read the magazine; so often the piece sent in is too long, or too short, or of a genre that we don't run – unless you actually make a pitch of that and say "I know you don't usually run this sort of piece but . . .".'
>
> His former colleague on The Guardian, features editor Alan Rusbridger, sighingly agrees. 'What makes the heart sink is the sheer amount of wasted effort by an army of people who submit pieces all over the place with a scattergun effect. Ninety per cent of the stuff would have no possible relevance. If only they could see what happens: it doesn't get beyond a highly-trained secretary.'

Approaching the editor

Magazines do receive a great many unsolicited articles; *New Society* used to get about 50 a week. Nearly all, if not absolutely all, of these would be unsuitable. People would, for instance, send in

10,000-word articles when the magazine rarely published anything over 2,000. Editors can tell from a glance at the first page – or even the first paragraph – whether the article is even remotely possible. Usually that glance is quite enough to reveal that it is written in completely the wrong style or concerns a topic inappropriate to the magazine. A woman's magazine doesn't want an article beginning 'The superstructure of Britain's economy reflects the influence of the current Kondratieff wave . . .'; an intellectual magazine doesn't want one with an opening 'Plasma physics is hot, hot, hot right now . . .'. Although this is a bit of an exaggeration, it isn't much – the mismatch between what is submitted and the nature of the magazine can be really quite startling.

Given that you have done your initial research and have an idea of the nature of the magazine and whom to contact, do *not* ring up. It might be a bad time; the editor could just have been shouting at them, they could be racing for a deadline or an appointment. It puts the journalist too much on the spot. It *would* be OK to phone if you have already written for the magazine and the journalist you are ringing knows your work. But for your first approach, the best procedure is to write a letter to the overall editor or a section editor, asking if they would be interested in a piece on your research, and describing it in two crisp paragraphs.

Describing your research so briefly can and should be a salutary experience. It forces you to focus on the central thrust of what may have been years of research, in a way that makes it sound interesting to the public and in particular, the target audience of that particular magazine. The bottom line is that if you can't make your work sound like a tempting story in two paragraphs, you are unlikely to be able to write an interesting article about it for public (as opposed to your colleagues') consumption. A brief statement such as 'My research shows that the earth's wobble is getting worse; this has striking implications for climatic conditions in the future' may be the result of ten years' work, thousands of measurements and calculations, and an analysis of a huge complex of factors. To boil it down can be painful. One way is to imagine that you've just met a complete stranger, whom you want to impress, at a cocktail party. 'What research do you do?' they ask. You sense you have 30 seconds to provide such a fascinating answer that they will be glued to your side for the rest of the evening, longing for details. *That's* how you have to sell your research to journalists.

Approaching the magazine by letter means that you won't waste your time writing an article that's totally unsuitable or unwanted, and if the editor does say that he or she would be interested in seeing it, it means they're prepared for it and will give it a bit of extra consideration.

What if your article is turned down? If a magazine turns you down, this is not a reason for automatic despair. You can be turned down for many reasons which do not reflect on the quality of the article. It may, for instance, be that, although they were interested in it, when they saw it it turned out simply to be not quite right for them. Each publication has its own style, and sometimes an editor may judge that the piece doesn't quite fit in with the magazine's 'feel' (and that sub-editing won't do the trick). If this seems to be the problem, then it is worth thinking about whether the article as written is more suited to another magazine, or whether you should rewrite it in the style of another magazine and send it there.

However, to maximize the chances of your first choice magazine taking the piece, it is vital that you study its writing style to get the level right. When writing, keep the audience constantly in mind, perhaps picking one representative figure if necessary – your mother, your best friend, a complete stranger who is female and in her twenties and whom you might meet on the bus. Whoever. But don't make the easily-committed mistake of talking down to any of them.

Points to bear in mind

- Always think *what is the story* here?
- What central point(s) am I trying to get across? This will prevent you rambling freely all over the topic, and focus your mind on what the *audience* might be interested in.

Many people tend to write for popular publications as though they are talking to themselves, describing all the things they personally find thrilling. They may also write for their colleagues, who might find, say, an illuminating slant on the latest theory. But an audience of laypeople will find these aspects totally snoozeworthy or irrelevant. People want to hear about things that relate to their own lives or are simply intrinsically interesting. The possible fate of the universe is interesting; the latest microtwist on superstring theory is not. A new, subtle development of the psychology of social judgment is not interesting; why we place such store on first impressions is.

Style. Writing for the public as opposed to one's colleagues means, for most scientists, a major shift in style.

The first shift is keeping sentences short. The academic style of long, convoluted sentences has to go. The use of these seems to be based on the assumption that if you don't cram each sentence full of about 20 subordinate clauses no one will take you seriously. Writing for non-colleagues means the frequent use of the full stop!

For magazines as much as any other media, it is vital not to use jargon. The exception is if you need to use a jargon word or phrase as a frequent label for a concept that it would be wordy and laborious to keep redescribing. In such a case, if you really can't avoid it, explain it in brackets the first time you use it.

The writing style needs to be lively and active (see also *Chapter 5* on press releases). In the early 1980s, a very well-known American journalist, Daniel Goleman (who has a PhD in clinical psychology from Harvard and was then senior editor on the magazine *Psychology Today*), offered hints on 'reader-friendly writing' which actually applies to all scientists. His speech was reported in the American Psychological Association's monthly newspaper *APA Monitor*:

> He [Goleman] said that he, too, had to overcome 'journalese disease', the symptoms of which include using long Latin words instead of punchy Anglo-Saxon terms [call a fruit fly, a fruit fly], passive rather than active voice, an impersonal tone ('one may find . . .'), abstract phrasing and jargon. He offered numerous examples of the problem:
>
> 'Of great theoretical and practical importance' means 'interesting to me';
>
> 'It is suggested that' means 'I think' and 'it is generally believed that' means 'a couple of other guys think so, too';
>
> 'Correct within an order of magnitude' really means 'wrong'.

In other words, don't lose the reader in a linguistic fog.

The first paragraph is the most vital. If readers are not hooked by that, they won't bother to read on. Introductions to magazine articles are unlike newspaper news stories, where the kernel of the story has to be in the first paragraph. You can start with an example or an anecdote in a magazine feature; anything vivid and gripping to hook the reader. If you're going to write about the psychological factors in pilot error, say, then start with something like, 'It was 9.09 p.m. on 17 January when the Boeing 707 ploughed into a Mauritian volcano, killing 202 people' rather than 'Pilot error is estimated to be a contributory factor in the majority of aircraft crashes'. By the time they make it to the full stop (if they do) the readers will be in a profound sleep.

Clarity. Keep everything simple and clear – avoid ambiguities. If a point is ambiguous, you can bet your last sock that the reader will either get hold of the wrong end of the stick or start to feel lost.

It is important to follow the argument through, and not to jump about. This can be hard when you want to say a lot in a short space, but the fact is that you are never going to be able to say all that you could have if you were given an unlimited word length. It's better to choose a clear thread of argument. The whole process is a bit like fishing – you hook the readers, then have to keep them on your line and pull them along. If the worst comes to the worst and you can't see a way of avoiding a rather bad gear change, try to smooth it over linguistically. You can do this, for example, by 'stitching' – repeating in the first sentence of a paragraph a word that appeared in the last sentence of the previous paragraph.

For example:

> . . . *The effects of divorce on children, then, are less dire than they have been painted by the media.*
>
> *The idea that divorce is increasing because we all expect more from marriage . . .*'

Stitching gives a sense of 'flow' even over a bit of a conceptual leap. If the piece loses its flow, the reader will slip off the fishing line and turn the page.

Quotes and anecdotes. Most magazines like quotes – they relieve the look of the copy. Otherwise, the text can look like great, off-putting slabs of unrelieved print. The mere presence of quotation marks lightens the look of the piece, and provides some variation in tone. At the shortest, a quote need only be a phrase in a sentence; it doesn't have to be a huge paragraph. For instance, 'Nuclear power plants, as Dr Snooks has pointed out, are "staggeringly risky technological environments"'.

Anecdotes and concrete examples to illustrate points are vital. Be specific wherever possible. So, for instance, if you're describing an alcohol experiment, mention that vodka/lager/dry martini-on-the-rocks was used. In a study of eccentrics say that 25% collected stuffed gerbils and 10% adored their mothers-in-law. Specifics help to liven up the copy and make what you're talking about more real. A great abstract outpouring is not what's wanted.

Length. A final point always to bear in mind is to keep the article to length. You should have agreed the length with the commissioning editor beforehand, and must stick to it. If it goes way overlength, it will be irritating and cause a great deal of work for the editor who has to cut it down. They may even decide that they cannot spare the time. You also risk it being cut in a way you dislike. If anyone is to cut it to length, it should be you before you send it in.

Presentation. Articles should of course be typed, with double line spacing (this leaves room for editing marks). Put your full name on the first page, and your surname and the page number at the top right hand corner of subsequent pages – 'BLOGGS – 3'. Type '/more' or '/mf' (more follows) at the bottom right hand corner of each page, and '/ends' at the end of the piece. All this ensures that, if the pages get separated in the heaving mass of paper on the editor's desk, the article can be put together again. It also does look professional, and as though you have made some study of what is required. Given the vast amounts of unsolicited bits of the world's forests that pass over editors' desks, anything that signals that you have made an effort to find out what the magazine needs – and haven't just produced a stream of consciousness in the bath – will help.

In your letter accompanying the article, you can provide a bit of extra information if you wish. Specifically, if there are things you could have put in the feature but didn't because of lack of space, you can always put them in a paragraph in the letter. For example, 'I also looked at the effect of the earth's wobble on the rainforests, but did not put it in for reasons of length. If you would like something on that, please let me know.' Then, if the article is not quite right, the editor has an idea of what else could be done with it.

Adjustments to your text. If your article is accepted, you must be prepared for the fact that it will be sub-edited. Even very experienced journalists get their copy subbed, so don't be offended. Subbing mainly happens to get pieces to length, to make them clearer or more readable, and to fit the magazine's style more closely. The sub-editors also have to adjust the text to the magazine's house style in terms of use of single and double quotation marks, whether per cent is written as '%' or 'per cent' and so on.

It may sometimes be that the editor or section editor thinks the article needs a major rewrite. They will, as we have seen, sometimes do it themselves, because they feel that it contains interesting information and is salvageable. Or they may return it to you to do, with detailed comments about what is wrong (from their point of view) with it. At worst, they may reject it. Again, do not be too upset. That happens to seasoned journalists too, even where an article has been commissioned. When you as a non-journalist start to write for magazines, you will not be commissioned, because they do not know your work. If they like your idea, they will invite you to send in the article on spec, with no redress if they reject it.

After one article has been accepted, however, you may expect the next one to be commissioned. This means that you will agree a fee for the piece before submitting it, which will be paid if it is published. If it is rejected, because you have been commissioned you will be paid at the very least a 'kill fee', probably about half the fee originally agreed and sometimes you will be paid in full.

Timing your submission

On weekly magazines, the last day for news copy is normally Monday for Thursday publication, and Tuesday for Friday publication. For features, the process is usually more leisurely. Indeed, unless there is a 'time peg', weeklies can sit on a feature for a long time before publication. The reason for this is that they build up a collection of stories and pick articles out of the pile as necessary to get a good mix of topics that week. A few serious, a few lighter, not two on the same topic – those sort of considerations. On *New Society*, for example, it was not unknown for a researcher to ring in and say diffidently (or furiously, depending on personality and desperation to be published) 'You've had my article for 18 months – are you still intending to publish it?'

The truth is that if a magazine keeps a feature too long, then probably there is something about it that stops it ever being picked out of the feature pile to be published that week. So don't let editors sit on your work for months on end. It is reasonable to assume that you will hear their verdict in about six weeks; if not, it's fair to ring. If the article is accepted, and has not appeared in say three to four months, then another call would be seen as reasonable.

If you possibly can, go for a time peg. This means that you link your article with some topical event. For example, when I was on the staff of *New Society*, I wanted to write a feature on the psychology of eyewitness testimony. There was a lot of new and exciting research around. But how to persuade the editor to put it into the magazine sooner rather than later? Suddenly, providence decreed that Parliament was going to have one of its periodic votes on hanging. And that was it – the article appeared in double-quick time as a cover story under the heading 'What if we hanged the wrong man?' Earthquakes, space probes, forensic enquiries, solar eclipses, floods, sunshine, even Valentine's Day, have all been used as pegs on which to hang science features.

The timing on monthly magazines is, as you might imagine, greatly extended. The last possible day for the submission of copy is about two months before publication. Most features would already be set by then, and sometimes even several months before. A time peg for the monthlies, then, is not such a feasible proposition. Interest value alone has to win the day.

Magazines need interesting features constantly. Since they are more features-oriented than hard news-oriented, magazine even more than newspaper journalism is an endless, desperate search for ideas. This might sound paradoxical; that they throw so much stuff in the bin and are still in dire need of ideas. But it's actually not, since most of the press releases and unsolicited articles (and sometimes solicited ones) that magazines receive are simply unusable – endless press releases on the latest anti-ageing cream, 12,000-word articles on cockroach mating habits in Outer Mongolia, that sort of thing.

Scientists have a major outlet for their work in magazines; editors, after all, have pages to fill. They need you.

4 RADIO & TV

Radio or TV? □ *Getting to know the media* □ *What's on radio?* □ *What's on TV?* □ *The editorial process* □ *Different contributions* □ *Local radio and TV* □ *Concepts* □ *Things people worry about*

With an ever-expanding web of television and radio providers and the apparent decentralization of the production of programmes to independents, it looks on the face of it like a pretty confusing maze for the humble scientist to enter. It is not. Indeed, it is really quite easy to decide what outlets are suitable for your work and how you should pitch your contribution. It involves a lot of listening to radio and watching television.

If you are inexperienced, never put yourself in the position of agreeing to take part in a programme with which you are totally unfamiliar. Programmes vary a lot in content and tone and a cosy sofa-sitting chat on a breakfast TV show requires a different approach from that needed for a serious radio programme such as *The World at One* on BBC Radio 4.

Radio or TV? Which Do You Approach?

Should you try to attract the attention of radio or television for a piece of research? Does the nature of the research have any influence on the outlet you target?

As a general rule, television has an obvious requirement which radio lacks – it needs pictures. Producers and directors are loathe to spend too much time filming a 'talking head' only, however good the story, whereas, of course, radio consists only of talk. Its pictures are generated by your words.

So, if you do approach television, be prepared to enter into discussions about what can be used to illustrate your concepts. If you have a sparkling new piece of equipment or an image of a recently discovered supernova to offer, there is no problem. The difficulties arise when you have to get others to visualize chemical reactions or mathematical conundra without the aid of expensive computer graphics. Contrary to popular misconception, TV companies do not lavish vast sums of money on everything they broadcast, especially if it is only a news 'short'.

By and large, though, it is up to you whether you approach your local radio or TV company with a story. Certainly a radio interview is quicker to give and less disruptive of your working day. On the other hand, TV has immense power to catch people's attention and is watched by a surprising number of people at all times of the day.

Getting to Know the Media to Which You Wish to Contribute

If you want proactively to project yourself into programmes, rather than waiting for invitations to come along, look through a television and radio guide such as the *Radio Times* and make notes on those programmes and producers with a science interest. It is better to call someone (or write or fax) by name. To find contacts, buy a copy of *The Blue Book of British Broadcasting* which tells you who does what and where in radio and television. Again, it is better to write to 'Jean Smith' than to 'The Station Manager' if you want to explore possibilities in local radio.

Science broadcasters in the UK represent a fairly small coterie and, with work, you could get to know who most of them are. Your university or learned society press or public affairs office should be of help in this. Indeed it is their job to keep tabs on the media – broadcast and print. Together you can build up a valuable database.

What's on Radio?

Here is a quick guide to the regular output of the BBC in the area of radio science. These are all programmes 'dedicated' to science, but, of course, many others carry science, medicine or technology items such as news broadcasts (including *Today*), and more general magazine programmes such as *You and Yours* or *Woman's Hour* have science slots. Other specialist programmes such as *In Touch* and *Does He Take Sugar?* also feature technology relevant to their target audiences. Here though are the science-based productions.

The main science programmes

- *Science Now*, *Medicine Now* and *The Parts* are, respectively, general science, clinical medicine and technology magazine programmes, all on Radio 4 (LW 198 kHz, FM 92.4–92.8). They originate in London at Broadcasting House. *Science Now* runs 52 weeks a year; *Medicine Now* 40 weeks; *The Parts* around two 8-week runs per year.

- *Formula 5* is a lively pop science show aimed at younger audiences. This originates from Broadcasting House on Radio 5 (693 and 909 kHz, 433 and 330 m).

- *Science Friction* (Radio 4) is a discussion-style programme on areas of controversy in science and medicine. It is an occasional series.

- *Blue Skies* on Radio 3 (FM 90.2–92.4) runs monthly and discusses issues at the meeting point of arts and science – 'science in a broad cultural context'.

- *The Litmus Test* is a science quiz, originating in Edinburgh for Radio 4.

- *The Natural History Programme* is what it says it is. Broadcast on Radio 4, it originates in the Natural History Unit, Bristol.

- Another regular series now on Radio 4 is the psychology and psychiatry magazine *All in the Mind*.

World Service Output. The regular World Service output is namely: *Science in Action* (weekly magazine); *Discovery* (ditto but with fewer items in greater depth); *New Ideas* (in technology); *Health Matters*; *Global Concerns* (environment).

Alongside these is a vast range of other programmes, not specifically science-based, broadcast by the BBC World Service, some in English, some in foreign languages. All are on the lookout for stories and may include items on science, technology and medicine.

Local media. The number of science outlets is swollen by the local radio network. The BBC and the independent sector combined offer a total number of stations of all kinds (including community radio) approaching 200. They all have one thing in common; they are small and sparsely resourced. This means that they have minimal research facilities and little time and money to spend on travelling around and paying contributors. It will therefore surely be useful for you or your press officer to make local contacts in order

to augment the station's limited resources and offer readily accessible stories that are of local interest.

One researcher has gone one better. He regularly interviews
other researchers in his university and edits these interviews into a
form suitable for his local radio station, becoming the *de facto*
science reporter for that station.

In fact, independent activity in the radio industry is on the
increase. The BBC is already commissioning and broadcasting programmes produced by groups who are not in-house staff
members. Like television, radio may end up having 25% of its
output produced in this way. This means that there is yet another
tranche of journalists out there hungry for stories and bringing an
injection of creative thinking into the broadcasting process. This
can only be good for you, as a source of scientific raw material.

What's on Television?

The general picture for science and technology on television is
similar to that for radio: there are opportunities in both specialist
programmes and non-specialist programmes for research to be
aired.

The predominantly science programmes are:

- *Tomorrow's World* on BBC 1 – weekly, primarily but not exclusively technology, with an emphasis on developments in engineering for the consumer. (This programme is often described as
  the 'whiz bang' show, in that if the science doesn't go 'whiz' or
  'bang' it doesn't get on.)

- *Horizon* on BBC 2 and *Equinox* on Channel 4 are hour-long,
  single-topic documentaries ranging over the whole of science.
  These provide an opportunity for producers to look in depth at
  any subject, including medical science and occasionally fringe
  science (such as the ubiquitous corn circles!).

- *QED*, on BBC 1, in 1993 entered its fourteenth season of films on
  science technology and medicine.

- Then there are regulars such as *Wildlife on One* which embraces
  current work in animal behaviour, and the astronomy veteran
  The Sky at Night. To this must be added *ad hoc* documentaries and

series such as *Life on Earth* and Channel 4's medical magazine *The Pulse* which began a first run of ten programmes in 1993.

Quite a lot of science finds its way into educational programmes at primary and secondary level, as well as into the enormous output of the Open University which is carried by BBC television.

Apart from these 'dedicated' programmes though, science inevitably crops up within the news context. BBC, ITV and Channel 4 each have specialist science correspondents (as does BBC Radio) who cover stories of the day in much the same way as newspaper journalists. They also endeavour to get their film reports on air – though, as is the norm in the news environment, they are competing for space with everything else that is happening in the world on a particular day. And even the best research in the world has trouble finding space when the Government loses a vote in the House of Commons or there is a terrorist bombing.

News magazines such as *Panorama*, *Public Eye*, or *World in Action* may also tackle scientific themes, especially when they have obvious relevance to the person in the street; genetic engineering, AIDS treatments, water pollution, and global warming are typically the sorts of subject matter you are likely to see on these programmes.

Television in Britain (and in most of the rest of the world for that matter) is often accused of giving science short shrift. On the face of it there seems some justification in the accusation in that no channel seems willing – with a few exceptions built around a major 'personality' – to give great airtime to research. However, in the general run of things, science does not do all that badly. It has had regular outlets for many years, and the programmes are usually broadcast at accessible times of the day to capture younger audiences. Television has also experimented quite a bit with new formats, for example, setting one magazine series in a travelling marquee.

The signs are that producers are ever-hungry for new research and new ways to present it on television.

Independent commissioning. In the last decade of the 20th century television in the UK is undergoing a revolution in terms of how programmes are made, as well as unprecedented growth.

The two BBC channels and the independent network, plus Channel 4, may soon be joined by a new national network, Channel 5, a whole host of satellite channels and a surge of cable broadcasting. This mushrooming should mean more opportunities for scientists to present their work both within news and individual programmes, but whether this will happen only time will tell.

Programme making is also in a state of flux. Until the arrival of Channel 4, all programmes were made in-house. Heads of department, editors, producers and directors fought within their respective companies for the annual allocation of air-time and then they generated their own programme ideas and made the actual programmes we saw. Today, the system is changing fast, with fewer programmes and programme ideas emanating from the central broadcasting companies. Independent production is the order of the day and for the future.

The Channel 4 science series *Equinox* is a good exemplar of how the system works. Once Channel 4 has decided it wants a science strand, and once air-time has been allocated, then the commissioning editor has the responsibility of ensuring that the appropriate number of programmes are made and ready for broadcast. The commissioning editor has two basic systems at his or her disposal. The first is to commission a single independent company to generate ideas and to make all the programmes for the series.

This system is commonly used for current affairs slots as well as magazine-type programmes. The second system is to approach a whole gamut of independent production companies and ask them to produce, in the first instance, a set of programme ideas, outlines, treatments. All these paper outlines are then sorted and selected and the lucky companies get to produce, usually, no more than one programme of the forthcoming *Equinox* series.

Although this system is enormously wasteful of ideas, as the commissioning editor at Channel 4 probably has about ten times more outlines than can ever be used, it is cheap in production terms as Channel 4 doesn't have to permanently employ whole rafts of editorial and production staff. The other advantage is that, supposedly, Channel 4 gets a wider trawl of programme ideas. Whether this is true or not, of course, is an untestable hypothesis.

This system of programme commissioning has now been imported to the BBC which has set itself a target of 25% of programmes to be made by independent external companies. The various regionally-based ITV companies also are moving in this direction, although more slowly, and Channel 5, when it comes on stream, will greatly depend on the independent production sector.

Although making predictions is a dangerous pastime, the shift away from in-house production is so inexorable that by the year

2010 in excess of 80% of TV programmes will be bought in from the independent sector.

The news. The system(s) described holds true for all individual programmes and series except for 'The News'. All the major broadcast companies have their own news-gathering and production staff and all decisions about what to cover are made in-house. (Although Channel 4 actually buys in its news service from Independent Television News (ITN), the same company that produces the news programmes for ITV). Each of the various regional companies that comprise the ITV network also have their own news gathering and output services.

There have been a couple of changes recently in this TV news sector, which are worthy of comment. First, at the BBC there is now an integrated news room for both TV and radio. Basically, this means that there is now a pool of specialist and generalist reporters who generate news stories, or are told what to cover, for either the radio or TV networks. Although the system sounds quite revolutionary the BBC have retained the system of a single editor for each of their programmes – *Today*, *World at One*, *The Six O'Clock News*, *The Nine O'Clock News* – so potentially it is still possible for the individual programmes/bulletins to be far from integrated.

The second recent change is within the ITV network. In 1992 all the ITV companies' franchises were up for auction, and new or existing companies were licensed to broadcast in their regional patches, for the next decade, up to 2003. News coverage figured prominently in all the franchise bids. Most of the companies cover quite large regional areas and criticism had been raised that the old companies only ever covered stories in and around their headquarters city. But this is changing. Many of the ITV companies now have two, three or four separate news gathering centres around a region and several are now splitting their broadcasting into regional sub-divisions in order to give their viewers a majority of local news.

This concept is only the TV version of a local newspaper and it is to be welcomed as, at a stroke, it has doubled or trebled the amount of ITV local news airtime that has to be filled – and why not by you and your research? The changing face of TV, both in general programmes and in the news, should open up more potential opportunities for the diligent scientist and/or researcher.

The newer independent production companies bidding for known slots are always open to and on the lookout for both new ideas and individuals to act as consultants. Finding these companies can be a bit of a pain, as some only last as long as the programme they are making. But the more reputable companies stick around and details on them can be found in the annual PACT *Directory of British Film and Television Producers*.

On the news side the process is simple and straightforward. Find out the various news rooms that cover your area and tell them what you are doing and give them your stories.

The Editorial Process: How Items Get Broadcast

There are, as you might expect, many similarities in the item-gathering process between broadcast and print journalism. Both are constantly seeking stories with a strong news slant. Both rely on original sources of research for their information.

A typical magazine programme on radio or television will scour press releases, conference programmes, journals and other printed materials such as laboratory or university research bulletins for likely leads. Researchers, producers or reporters will attend press conferences or other meetings where, again, it is essential that they get crucial information concisely and clearly.

Of course, one difference with radio or television is that a sound or film crew might also turn up at a press conference and expect to record something. Provision must be made for this. A radio interview needs a quiet room, undisrupted by the telephone for half an hour or so. Television set-ups and shoots usually take quite a bit longer. That has to be factored into the organization of the meeting. It is no use the chairperson saying, after a few questions from the press, 'Well, that's it, I'm afraid. I have to catch a train,' or 'Sorry, we can't give telly interviews'. (For more on press conferences see p. 98).

Broadcasters are journalists and a *bona fide* part of the press corps. As well as the regular routes of information gathering, all broadcasters have their own networks. People who have talked to the radio or TV about their research before might well call up the programme producer to offer their services for a follow-up. This is always worth doing and ongoing research stories are particularly appropriate for the specialist programme.

Freelancers. Many reporters are freelancers, working for both national and local stations. Some are more knowledgeable than others, but again, all are looking for stories. A goodly proportion of the best freelancers specializing in science are members of the Association of British Science Writers (ABSW, c/o British Association for the Advancement of Science, Fortress House, 23 Savile Row, London W1X 1AB).

The process of selecting individual items for broadcast is really no different from the process in any other part of the media. An editor or executive producer will have overall editorial control of the output. Working in collaboration with producers and researchers, he or she will formulate the mix of items based on a combination of intrinsic interest, quality, newsworthiness, availability of contributors and sheer expediency dictated by time constraints. There are no rules to the editorial game beyond that of human judgement about what will make for an entertaining, informative, and balanced show.

Rejection. Say, for example, you do everything absolutely correctly. You complete some excellent research, send out a perfectly-written media release or call a well-choreographed press conference. But, alas, the programme makers you thought would jump at your offering fail to give you air time. It happens. It happens because the editor feels it is not quite right in the week you went public. The programme may have had items on the chemistry of polymers or the pheromonal communication of insects for the previous two weeks running and a third would look like overkill.

More often you might actually record an interview which gets ousted (as happens with newspapers) by something hotter at the last minute. There is little you can do about this. Broadcasters hate to discard items because they take time to collect and edit. In fact it is very frustrating for them to lock up half a day or even more of the working week for something that is never aired. So both parties are pretty disgruntled. Such is the pattern of all journalism.

Different Types of Contribution

Radio – and to a slightly lesser extent television – is arguably the 'purest' form of media communication in that you the expert use your own words to communicate directly with your audience, cutting out the journalist/reporter in the middle.

Probably the commonest type of contribution made by scientists on radio or television is the straight interview. It may be in a news programme or sandwiched between records in a music and chat show or as part of a specialist magazine programme such as *Science Now* or *Discovery*.

Each interview is self-contained. Each is structured, having a beginning, middle and end, and will tell your story; that is, the findings from your research.

Documentaries and features. However, straight interviews are not your only voice in the media. You may for example be asked to take part in a documentary or feature. Here the procedures are much the same but the style is often quite different. Suppose, for example, the feature is on the fashion for facial cosmetic surgery. The producer will want contributions from individuals who have had such surgery, surgeons themselves and maybe a few psychologists with research interests in person/facial perception, social interaction, attitude to disfigurement and so on.

If you are one such 'expert' you may be asked quite a few questions, for well over half an hour, on topics that seem to 'jump around a bit'. The usual story structure is abandoned. The reason for this becomes clear when you hear or see the feature. Contributions from a number of people are often cut up and interposed one with another; sometimes a voice will appear merely to add a sentence reflecting on what has just been said or to pose a question that someone else will subsequently answer. A good feature or documentary relies on stitching together a variety of voices in a coherent fashion to tell a combined story. Your personal contribution may pop up several times within that framework.

Now there is little you can do to control what is or is not used here. You are very much in the hands of the producer. You have to trust him or her not to make you appear aggressive or egregious or quirky. It is no use asking, when you have just recorded your contribution – the 'raw material' – 'What bits will you use?' Realistically the producer probably cannot tell you. The bits will suggest themselves later when all the raw material has been listened to or seen and evaluated.

Phone-ins. Quite a different proposition is the phone-in. Here it is not so much your answers that are the problem but the questions. If you were a psychologist with expertise in person perception taking part in a phone-in on cosmetic surgery, you might well be tested quite vigorously. You might receive calls from a disfigured person, say, who cannot see why so much fuss and money is expended on minor cosmetic operations when some people have major blemishes to cope with; or a distraught individual who, having had cosmetic surgery, finds that life is not quite as entrancing as he or she hoped it would be. Instead of airing your knowledge of social psychology you might find yourself in the uncomfortable role of radio clinician. Thus, an energy expert can be lured into the problems of the developing world or the astronomer confronted by big questions of a metaphysical nature.

Remember that phone-ins are not consulting rooms or vehicles for saving the world but an opportunity for people to air their opinions, grievances and passions. You are not expected to give definitive answers, but to suggest routes to solutions. Indeed the dogmatic, know-all who has it all off pat does not make for good listening. You need to learn to *interact* with callers. Ask questions. Ask their views. Show enthusiasm for them as people. Be friendly.

In praise of surrogates

For the most part, scientists and engineers will usually be approached by radio and television producers to give a horse's mouth account of their own work. Sometimes though, if you have been successful talking about yourself, you may be asked to talk about the work of someone else. It may be work that lies within your own field, or it may be outside – perhaps some way outside – it.

Many researchers are reluctant to take on either role, especially if it is definitely outside their own sphere of interest. In fact, there have been relatively few media scientists happy to talk about, say, particle physics, phobic disorders, IQ tests, plant pathology, silicon chips and the mechanisms of black holes with any authority. 'Not my field' is a response with which all producers are familiar.

However, this caution is probably an overreaction. After all, when called on to describe another person's work you are not undergoing a PhD viva. You are simply restating the aims, methods and results in everyday language – acting as an interpreter of say an article in a scientific journal written by another hand. In other words, you do not need to be an expert to become an 'expert' for media purposes; you need to be informed and articulate, a kind of specialist reporter. This is a role a few researchers have tried with some success and enjoyment. It is a feature of the academic community that media academics who do turn their hand to almost anything tend to attract scorn and criticism from their peers. This is usually a manifestation of sour grapes, a secret thwarted wish to be in their place. Provided you stick to what you know and what you can assume from the facts, there is no dishonour in becoming a regular commentator on matters scientific, any more than there is in talking about politics or economics.

Of course, there is another argument in favour of being a regular performer. If you, as a trained and respectable scientist, are reluctant to speak out, some other, less creditable, individual might not be. Why deliver your discipline, your profession into the hands of ill-informed amateurs?

Local Radio and Television: Local Slant

Local radio and television aim to be just that – local in interest. They do not shun national or international issues but thrive on news and current affairs with a strong flavour of the community.

A local station can, like a national station, achieve this both reactively and proactively as far as science and technology are concerned. If a local river becomes polluted, or a power station goes on 'red alert' or all the city's traffic lights fail during rush hour, then someone from the area's scientific community could or should be called on to comment or analyse or clarify what went wrong. Researchers working on the environment, climate, energy supply and agricultural matters are frequent visitors to their local radio station.

Clearly though, any research department could be on the radio station's list for potential interviewees. Criminologists or psychologists might be asked to reflect on a spate of local crime; astronomers on alleged UFO sightings; economists on the poor attendances at the local beaches; epidemiologists on a local TB outbreak. If you are interested in becoming one of those regularly contacted for your views, you should:

- Make yourself known to the local station manager. Telephone first, ascertain his or her name, then follow up with a very brief sheet giving your name, telephone number(s), areas of expertise and interest.

- Keep abreast of local affairs. Usually, if the radio station does call asking to interview you, the reporter will be able to provide some details of the story in question. If you can dig deeper though, you will have more knowledge and authority than you would have simply doing an interview on the wing, without preparation.

Local radio is also a good forum for you to operate proactively, initiating stories that might appeal to a local audience. Here are some of the sorts of scientifically flavoured ideas that could well hit the local airwaves:

- A laboratory builds/unveils/starts work on an adventurous/ large/unusual piece of equipment.

- The first woman/disabled person/man is appointed to a local job in research.

- A researcher has results from a specifically local study on water quality/television watching/muesli consumption.

- Your department gets a tidy sum of money from a research council/charity/a local celebrity.

- Your department needs a tidy sum of money from . . . for . . . etc.

In all of these examples there is certainly room to air your research. You will find it easier to sell if you can exploit something that relates to the immediate experience of your audience. That's a general rule in any form of journalism. But it is virtually a *sine qua non* for local radio.

Concepts and Conceits

Radio, just as much as television, deals in pictures – images created in the minds of listeners. As an interviewee you have to fuel this need for graphic representation. As a researcher too you have to find ways of rendering the complexities of your branch of your discipline accessible to the lay person. Your route, in many cases, will be to use metaphor, simile, analogy and other kinds of imagery.

It is not always easy. Science in general has been slow to exploit the advantages of imagery that fiction writers have been using for centuries, probably because it is often hard to encapsulate research ideas in neat little comparisons. Many researchers are suspicious of images because they do not tell the whole story. They argue – understandably – that to describe for example a personality trait as a ' "Sword of Damocles" hanging over an individual's head' may be graphic but exaggerated; or to say that brain cell receptors act 'like locks and keys' gives only a crude analogy for an exquisitely refined biological mechanism. Even so, for all the limitations of imagery, it is worth trying to find graphic ways of rendering your research accessible. Here are a few tips.

■ *Anthropomorphism* is a useful ploy. The late Peter Medawar once raised a laugh by suggesting that the cosmos may have been 'too reticent' to begin with a Big Bang, while Primo Levi, industrial chemist cum author of *The Periodic Table* described one of his characters, namely stannous chloride, thus: 'It is aggressive but also delicate, like certain unpleasant sports opponents who whine when they lose'. A favourite of all time though is Richard Feynman's characterization of an elementary particle called a neutrino. It has nothing much going for it, little mass, no electric charge and just sort of lies around all the time doing nothing. 'As a prototype', quipped Feynman, 'think of your son-in-law!'

■ *Comparisons* are the scientific explicator's stock-in-trade. James Jeans in his wonderful book *The Mysterious Universe* captured the vastness of the heavens by estimating that there are as many stars in the sky as there are grains of sand on all the world's beaches. On the micro-scale you can picture the empty space that surrounds the nucleus at the heart of the atom as comparable to an orange in the middle of St Paul's Cathedral.

■ *Metaphors* are also useful in expressing concepts. It is a mistake to assume that 'gee-whizz' images are just for public consumption. Scientists frequently need to find mental pictures to express difficult concepts, and they draw these from everyday experience. When a fertilized egg cell begins to divide, multiply, proliferate, grow and take the form of an embryo, a very complex set of activities takes place involving cellular movement and communication. Cells seem to 'know' where they are meant to go. Some migrate to the end of the emergent hands to form fingernails, some eyes or lips, others organize themselves to make kidneys, heart and liver and so on.

So purposeful are these cellular migrations that it almost looks as if each cell has on board its own route map. Moreover each unit also seems able to stay in touch with other types of cell (using the original cellular phone, perhaps?) so that they do not interfere with each other's peregrinations. It all resembles the daily exodus of thousands of office workers pouring out of the city at 5.30 p.m., and finding, unerringly, their individual way home to Orpington, Islington or Wembley, then to Flat B, 117, Acacia Drive.

One biologist studying the intricacies of the developing embryo considers this kind of everyday metaphor helpful in his research work. By reducing complex genetic and biochemical niceties to some mundane notion such as the commuter's journey across the city, he comes both to appreciate better the scientific problems that face him and to hit on new ways of resolving them.

So, in finding your own scientific metaphors you may, in fact, be enhancing your own understanding of your subject matter.

Things People Worry About

'I've got a Brummie/Cockney/Glaswegian accent'

It is undoubtedly a relic from the early days of broadcasting that people often associate a 'radio voice' with the cut-glass, upper-middle-class tones of BBC announcers circa 1945. The fact is there is no such thing as a 'good' radio or TV accent, only good broadcasters. Think of Jacob Bronowski with his deliberate, heavily accented delivery. He made scientific points with such conviction and erudition that what should have been a handicap became a positive virtue.

Regional accents, personal mannerisms, idiosyncrasies even, are all permissible. Broadcasters do not discriminate against anyone because he or she obviously comes from a particular part of the UK, or indeed anywhere else in the world. Accents or mannerisms are only a problem when they impair communication. The same holds true for a pronounced stammer. If you have a speech impediment of any kind, especially the sort that tends to manifest itself under pressure, make the fact known before you are interviewed. If the interview is pre-recorded, it is often possible to edit out the worst patches. The producer will probably be able to judge from talking to you whether this will be appropriate for you.

Nervousness can also alter your voice. Under stress people tend to talk more quickly and at a higher pitch. A few deep breathing exercises in the loo before you start the interview will help to relax you and keep your voice at a pleasant even pace.

'Are you going to edit this?'

Many would-be interviewees shrink from the media because they fear the sharp cut of the editorial razor blade. They worry that a skilful but unscrupulous producer will misrepresent, distort or even wilfully contradict what they have been saying by re-arranging words. Now while it is true that it is not difficult to omit or re-shuffle words and phrases to turn common sense into gobbledegook, or an affirmative into a negative, this is not what editing is all about.

Editing is a cosmetic process: the cleaning up of unwanted trivia or irrelevance to make speech flow more smoothly. It takes two forms. First comes the excision of the many 'ums' and 'ers' which pepper everyday speech; this process is known as 'de-umming'. There are good psychological reasons for introducing these little sounds into our conversation: they give us time to think, to emphasize, to prevaricate and so on. In the real world they usually go unnoticed.

However, on radio 'umming' and 'erring' can be quite enervating, just as it would if written down verbatim in, say, a conversation in a novel. By literally cutting the tape before and after the 'er' and sticking the ends together, radio editing can transform a very tedious or disjointed flow of speech. The same is done for the constant pauses, repetitions, 'I means', 'How shall I put its' and many other everyday linguistic devices that do not actually say anything.

The second level of editing is editing-for-content. Here the idea is to add pace and directness to a narrative by judicious trimming of conditionals, reservations, asides and back-tracking. Consider these two examples. First, an unedited piece of interview, as recorded with no intervention at all by the broadcaster.

'So what we came up with, I mean the sort of suggested results we derived from the initial data analysis, was a – a kind of – er – how shall I put it, well a sort of series of contradictions. Paradoxes almost, though not paradoxes in the classical sense – though that would have been satisfying . . . anyway what we ended up with was . . . '.

Now for the edited version with takes appreciably less time to convey the meaning.

'What we came up with was a series of contradictions. . . '.

Now you could argue that flavour, tone and attitude are lost in the editing. But listeners want facts not embroidery. Editing helps to deliver them neatly and speedily.

Sometimes interviewees will ask whether they can hear the edited version of an interview before it is broadcast. Usually, though not invariably, this request is refused. The reason is not that the broadcaster wants *carte blanche* to edit recklessly without giving you a chance to correct any errors or distortions. It is rather a practical one. Often in making programmes – especially news, current affairs and magazine programmes – a producer will have to make rapid cuts in the taped material to get it to fit a time slot. Under pressure, he or she may well cut quite deeply into your taped interview while the programme in which it occurs is actually being transmitted. So the producer cannot in all honesty let you hear or see the 'final' version until it is broadcast, by which time it is too late anyway to take corrective action.

Strange language

'Right, Paul. Stick a blonde over in that corner and see whether we've got a couple more redheads in the van. Oh and while you're there, I need some better sticks'.

A television crew speaks a strange language. What seems like a prelude to the flagellation of some young ladies is nothing of the sort. The 'blondes' and 'redheads' are the names of commonly-used lights while the camera operator's call for better 'sticks' simply means that a tripod needs replacing.

The hustle and bustle of setting up a location shoot – say in your office – can be disturbing, especially when it is carried out in an unknown technospeak. Inexperienced performers are often puzzled, particularly by 'noddies'. What are these all about –and is Big Ears involved?

A 'noddy' is an extra sequence filmed mute (no sound running) in which the interviewer will look at you or even a blank wall while the camera records his or her reactions – nods, smiles, frowns, a hint of resignation and so on. These shots are edited into the interview to give emphasis, visual relief and to cover junction points. Sometimes you will be asked to chat away with your interviewer, again mute, while the camera records, from a different angle, a wider shot – a 'two shot'. Again this is needed to inject relief, to cover an edit in the interview and, often, to act as an establishing shot at the very opening of the broadcast interview.

The main thing to remember is that the setting up and lighting of these cosmetic touches takes time. Thus, although you may have cracked through your interview in one brilliantly-timed 'take', you cannot escape to the canteen for at least another hour or so until the inevitable noddies have been put in the can.

One last bit of terminology. In both radio and television production you will often hear someone asking for something 'wild'. It is not an invitation to an interesting kind of party, but an extra piece of material to help in editing. Sound recordists take 'wild track' of the background ambience of the room in which the interview is recorded in order to facilitate editing or to give the production team greater flexibility in how they use their raw interview material.

'I'll call you back'. Human beings are self-effacing, obliging creatures. Someone treads on your toe in the street and you say you're sorry. A producer or journalist calls you on the telephone asking you to comment on someone's research with which you are barely familiar and you feel you simply have to oblige them with a detailed, erudite answer.

However, if you are unfamiliar with radio or television work, do not be in too much of a hurry to say 'yes' to the first person to invite you to take part in a programme. Find out what is wanted/ expected of you and if you have any reservations at all ask for some thinking time. Say you will call back in 15 minutes, by which time you will:

a) have decided properly whether you want to take the plunge; or
b) have formulated a few more searching questions.

Do not be afraid to ask for thinking time. If they want you and value you, they'll wait.

The question of fees. Unless you are one of the megastars of television science, do not expect to retire early as a result of your contact with the broadcast media. Even so, do expect to be paid if you give an interview or allow your laboratory to be used as a 'facility'. Think though in terms of £30, £50 or £100 chunks rather than the sort of sums you would need to have paid into a numbered account in a Swiss bank. It is up to you to ascertain what is on offer for your contribution and to ensure that you get your expenses paid if travel and hotels are involved.

You will probably be asked to sign some sort of contract giving permission for your contribution to be used as the broadcaster thinks fit. This is a pretty standard affair hardly justifying seeking legal advice, unless there is a clause that has the potential for conflict with another contract you may have signed – say with a publisher or an employer.

Facility fees – for disrupting your lab for a day – are often negotiated by your university or laboratory finance people direct. You should obviously talk to them in advance if you want to make any special arrangements with the radio or TV company, say for diverting funds to a charity.

Should you be called on to be more than a straightforward interviewee, perhaps to write and present a documentary or even a series, the guidelines for fees become less clear. There are no set rates for being a presenter: these are often negotiated by agents and can vary enormously.

Perhaps the best way is for you to make some estimate of your daily rate (the sort of money you could earn doing something else such as consultancy or teaching) and then ask your producer to estimate how many days he or she realistically wants you to work. You may end up by agreeing a figure you can both live with.

If you are working for the BBC the process is a bit more simple in that the BBC has a range of standard fees from which it will offer you a sum automatically. You are not obliged of course to accept this but, by and large, there is relatively little leeway if you are going to haggle.

•   •   •

Finding your way around radio and TV then, both in terms of the outlets available for your stories and your working relationship with the media, is very much an empirical exercise. The more contacts you make, the more familiar the territory will become. The main thing is – if you have not already done so – to dip your toe in the water.

5 MEDIA RELEASES

Attracting media attention □ *Components of a successful media release*
□ *Design* □ *Distribution* □ *Timing* □ *Composition*

Releases can be the bane of a journalist's life. Every day of the year the science correspondent will receive hundreds of releases. Probably well over 90% will only receive a cursory glance; the journalist may never get beyond the stage of registering who sent the release and its headline. Of the rest, the journalist will probably not read beyond the first sentence or two, and perhaps as few as 2 or 3% will be read *in toto*. But conversely, the media release is also one of the best sources of information for the journalist, and probably more scientific stories get written or broadcast via this route than any other. So the importance of getting it right must be recognized.

Media releases come in two basic forms. The first is the 'news style' (see *Figure 5.1*) which aims to ape a news story exactly as it would appear in a (national) newspaper. The second is the 'teaser' (see *Figure 5.2*). This style provides only the bare bones of a story to whet the appetite of the journalist and to force the recipient to find out more. Often this style will leave questions deliberately unanswered, hoping that they are so vital that the journalist will be driven to investigate. The 'teaser' is more difficult to construct and write and has the inherent dangers that the journalist will say 'So what?', or simply not have the time to follow it up. So, beware the 'teaser' release; it can backfire.

The journalism trade press often contains rants about the standards of press release writing. Many of these complaints are quite justified and, as was said earlier, the poorly-produced release is a waste of everyone's time. Examples of bad release-writing are easy to find, but they are unlikely to teach us anything except how to write badly. The remainder of this chapter will concentrate on the 'news style' of media release and attempt to point out the lessons we need to learn to ensure that our stories get picked up and used.

Date: Thursday 6 December
Embargo: 14:00 hrs Tuesday 18 December

LUNCH-TIME PINT MAKES DRIVERS SLEEPY

Alcohol for women is more potent lunch-time than evening at impairing driving and vigilance. Even a single pint of beer could promote early afternoon sleepiness, with increased dangers for motorway drivers.

Professor Jim Horne, of Loughborough University, reported these findings today, Tuesday 18 December, at the London Conference of The British Psychological Society, held at City University. After consuming a moderate dose of alcohol at either lunch-time or early evening, his participants under-went vigilance tests and 40 minutes of monotonous motor-way driving in a car simulator.

Professor Horne, who is Director of the Sleep Research Laboratory, says, 'most drivers ought not to drink at all at lunch-time, and the legal blood alcohol limit is no guide to "safe" driving.'

FOR FURTHER INFORMATION: Contact Stephen White, Director of Information, The British Psychological Society. Telephone 0533 549568 (work), 0533 000000 (home) or . . .

DURING THE CONFERENCE (17/18 December): Telephone 071 490 2512/3.

Figure 5.1 An example of a 'news style' media release.

Date: Thursday 6 December
Embargo: 14:00 hrs Tuesday 18 December

THE EFFECTS OF ALCOHOL AT LUNCH-TIME

Does alcohol have a greater effect on driving skills at lunch-time or in the evening?

Professor Jim Horne, Director of the Sleep Research Unit at Loughborough University will discuss this issue at the London Conference of The British Psychological Society today, Tuesday 18 December, held at City University.

His research involved testing women after they had drunk four vodka and tonics either at lunch-time or in the early evening.

FOR FURTHER INFORMATION: Contact Stephen White, Director of Information, The British Psychological Society. Telephone 0533 549568 (work), 0533 000000 (home) or . . .

DURING THE CONFERENCE (17/18 December): Telephone 071 490 2512/3.

Figure 5.2 An example of a 'teaser' media release.

What Will Attract Media Attention?

The first prerequisite is that we have to have something to say, we have to have 'news' which we want to transmit to the public via the media. So what *is* news? Ask 50 journalists and you'll probably get 50 different answers. Dr David Whitehouse, Science Correspondent, BBC News and Current Affairs, said: 'I can't define what news is, but I know it when I see it'. That message is echoed by most journalists you ask. If this is taken together with the other oft-stated fact that what makes a news story today often wouldn't get into the papers either yesterday or tomorrow, what are the implications for us, the originators and disseminators?

As we can't predict which of our stories will 'make' on any given day then the guiding principle is – provide the journalists with as much original information as possible and let the media make the decisions. This message needs to be tempered a little, otherwise journalists will be swamped with paper they can never use. If you are responsible for the media relations for a large conference, then it would not be possible to write a media release on every single paper. So you have to be selective in terms of the papers you choose to release, but at the same time as sending the releases you should also send the full programme and (if possible) the abstracts, so that the journalists can assess for themselves the newsworthiness of other items.

A problem, particularly within science, is that if it isn't a brand new discovery at the leading edge of experimental work then we believe no one will be interested. This isn't true. Just because the research is slightly old hat within our own community doesn't necessarily mean that it will be familiar to the media – in fact you can almost guarantee that only a tiny minority will have heard of it. All the media needs to justify running 'old news' is a topical peg, such as someone said it 'yesterday' or a conference will discuss it 'next week'.

The media also appears to have a very short memory, or it is very ecologically minded, as re-cycling of stories happens regularly. So, if you had a story appear, in say January, there is nothing to stop you issuing an almost identical story in September. If it was a 'good story' then, it's likely to still be a 'good story', as long as you can find the new topical news peg. If there is some extra, or more recent, information in the new release so much the better. So, if we've got past the stage of deciding we've got a story, how can we put together a release that will attract the journalist?

The Four Components of a Successful Media Release

To get a release right, four separate elements have to be considered:

1. DESIGN   2. DISTRIBUTION   3. TIMING   4. COMPOSITION

Design

The design and layout of a release is almost as important as the words it contains. Remember what you are trying to do is produce

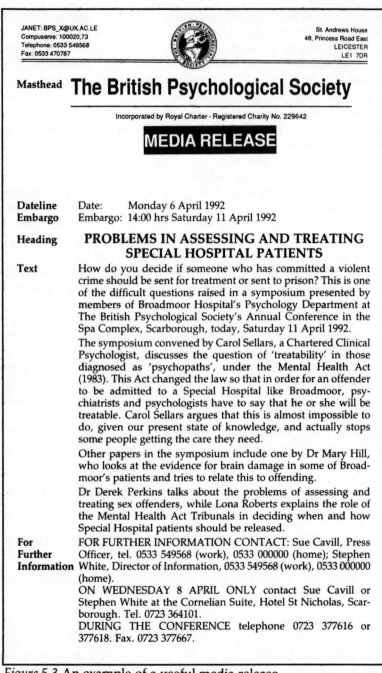

JANET: BPS_X@UK.AC.LE
Compuserve: 100020,73
Telephone: 0533 549568
Fax: 0533 470787

St. Andrews House
48, Princess Road East
LEICESTER
LE1 7DR

Masthead **The British Psychological Society**

Incorporated by Royal Charter - Registered Charity No. 229642

MEDIA RELEASE

Dateline	Date: Monday 6 April 1992
Embargo	Embargo: 14:00 hrs Saturday 11 April 1992

Heading

PROBLEMS IN ASSESSING AND TREATING SPECIAL HOSPITAL PATIENTS

Text

How do you decide if someone who has committed a violent crime should be sent for treatment or sent to prison? This is one of the difficult questions raised in a symposium presented by members of Broadmoor Hospital's Psychology Department at The British Psychological Society's Annual Conference in the Spa Complex, Scarborough, today, Saturday 11 April 1992.

The symposium convened by Carol Sellars, a Chartered Clinical Psychologist, discusses the question of 'treatability' in those diagnosed as 'psychopaths', under the Mental Health Act (1983). This Act changed the law so that in order for an offender to be admitted to a Special Hospital like Broadmoor, psychiatrists and psychologists have to say that he or she will be treatable. Carol Sellars argues that this is almost impossible to do, given our present state of knowledge, and actually stops some people getting the care they need.

Other papers in the symposium include one by Dr Mary Hill, who looks at the evidence for brain damage in some of Broadmoor's patients and tries to relate this to offending.

Dr Derek Perkins talks about the problems of assessing and treating sex offenders, while Lona Roberts explains the role of the Mental Health Act Tribunals in deciding when and how Special Hospital patients should be released.

For Further Information

FOR FURTHER INFORMATION CONTACT: Sue Cavill, Press Officer, tel. 0533 549568 (work), 0533 000000 (home); Stephen White, Director of Information, 0533 549568 (work), 0533 000000 (home).

ON WEDNESDAY 8 APRIL ONLY contact Sue Cavill or Stephen White at the Cornelian Suite, Hotel St Nicholas, Scarborough. Tel. 0723 364101.

DURING THE CONFERENCE telephone 0723 377616 or 377618. Fax. 0723 377667.

Figure 5.3 An example of a useful media release.

a piece of paper that is functional and of use to the recipient. So a useful media release should look something like the example in *Figure 5.3*. Let's go through all the design elements and examine why they are necessary.

Masthead. The first piece of communication which is vital is that the journalist must know the originating organization and that what they've received is a media release. These may seem ridiculously simplistic points but journalists receive hundreds of bits of paper without this basic information, and they then have to decide whether they have received a release, a letter for publication, or a private letter, and who the hell it is from. Your normal letterhead will probably do as long as you add the words 'Media Release'.

The consistent use of a masthead has another very important rationale. In the great plethora of releases in the journalist's in-tray each day, the sight of a recognizable masthead is like a lighthouse to a lost sailor. You can train a journalist to read your releases just by the sight of the masthead (it's called 'operant conditioning' in psychology). If in the past a journalist got a 'good story' from your source, then whenever your masthead pops into view the release will be read – and that's more than half the battle.

Dateline. This should be the date that you actually issue the release. Again, it has its use in that the journalist needs to know, at a glance, that the piece of paper is current and not something which can be instantly discarded.

Embargo. This line indicates the actual time and date of the event and says to the journalist 'you mustn't use this information before the time and date given'. The media like embargoes. First, because it gives them time to find some extra background if required, and second, because it stops competitors stealing a march. The breaking of embargoes by news organizations is rare, as they know that if they consistently do it then you, the originator, will stop sending those miscreants your releases. This is a serious sanction and one no journalist wants to be responsible for.

There is a debate in journalism about the time which should appear in the embargo line. The tradition is to use 00:01 (one minute past midnight) on the day of the event. This allows newspapers, radio and TV to report your event in that morning's editions – 'Dr So and So *will tell* a Royal Society meeting *today* . . .'.

However many journalists are now saying that they prefer the real time of the event to appear. This will result in the following day's papers reporting: 'Dr So and So *told* the Royal Society *yesterday* . . .' type story, although of course radio and TV will still be able to cover the story at any time after the embargo.

The real time embargo, especially for conferences, can actually persuade journalists to attend the event rather than doing all the work by phone in the one or two days before. Actually having a journalist in attendance improves your chances of coverage as the investment of money and time will have already been made.

Headline/heading. Very few of us have the skill to write Guardianesque headlines which will grab the attention of the readers, so be simple and write three, four or five words which factually state the subject of the release.

The text. The release should be no longer than one side of A4 (200–250 words maximum), double spaced and with a wide left margin. All these points have a reason. One side of A4 because no journalist has got time to read more. Even if your story ends up as an 800-word feature the writer will come to you for the extra information, so you don't need to provide any more than the nub of the news. Double spaced and wide left margin are essential so that editing marks can be put in the text and in the margin, and for ease of reading.

For further information. Again this is a vital element of any release. No matter how perfect your release, it is almost inevitable that, if the story is going to be used, the journalist will want to talk it through. So the names and numbers cannot be missed off. A home telephone number is a must. Journalists tend not to work office or 'scientist' hours, and early evening and Sunday mornings are prime times for them to call.

Distribution

You may have a beautifully designed and laid out release; you may have polished the words to perfection; you may even have a great story, but, unless you can get it to the right people at the right time, the whole exercise has been a waste of time. So the first piece of decision making is: who should receive your release, who could possibly use it, who would find your story/news/event of greatest interest?

Who should you send your release to? The natural first reaction, when releasing a 'science' story is to send it to the 'science correspondent'. But these specialists are few and far between and consequently they are deluged with more material than they can use across an enormously wide field. So we must try to use lateral thinking to target other correspondents who might be a better (and/or additional) target. Almost anything in the pharmaceutical and/or drug field should be of interest to the medical/health correspondent, as would epidemiological stories. The social affairs correspondent tends to be a good target for sociological and anthropological material, and child development and educational research material is obviously a must for the education correspondent. But to try to give any more than cursory guidance here may be misleading – what is needed for each and every release is to look carefully at the content and then target appropriately. This really only applies to the quality and middle-market national (and major regional) media, because the rest of the media doesn't employ the range of specialist correspondents, and for these the general advice is to address releases to the news editor.

Using your local media

If you are starting out in the media release business then start local. This means compiling a list of all your local media: newspapers both daily and weekly (and the freesheets); radio (both BBC and independent); the TV companies which cover your patch; any local press agencies; and any local freelance reporters. If you work in an academic department then your institution's Press Officer no doubt will already have good local lists (and potentially good national lists as well). Always check these lists over just in case your story is more appropriate for a different audience.

Scientists often forget about their local media and this is a great mistake. Firstly, the take-up of stories is likely to be greater than on the national scene; secondly, the more local material you have appearing then the closer the bonds between you and your local community; thirdly, and perhaps most importantly, it can be a cost-effective way of getting your story into the national media. Local papers, local radio and local TV all feed into their respective national networks and if the local media see the wider potential of your story then they will pass it on up the chain.

Starting in your own geographical neck of the woods has a further advantage. You can use it to train yourself gently in both the skills of release writing and the skills of appearing on local radio and being interviewed by the local newspaper. The local media journalists are unlikely ever to give you a hard time, because it is in their interest to 'keep you sweet' for future use – without you they lose a potential source.

Distribution to the national media was mentioned earlier (p. 79) but there are a couple of further points to note when you feel you are ready to release your story nationally. A trick used by many release distributors is to use a scatter-gun approach. They will identify the two, three or four specialist correspondents who may/ should be interested and send the release to all of them, plus a copy to both the news and the features editors. This may sound wasteful, but if your resources allow then it can be and is a successful strategy.

I haven't mentioned the national magazine market which is vast and diffuse (see *Chapter 3*). But before passing on, it is simply worth saying that there is a trade press in just about every conceivable area of activity and therefore your story potentially has a market in this sector. Specific science magazines are few and far between – *New Scientist* and *Nature* – but at the time of writing three separate publishers are planning to put a 'popular' science monthly on the newstands. Let's hope that at least one or two come to fruition so that we all have a few more straight science outlets for our material.

Using press agencies. Press agencies, both local and national, exist by selling stories to the rest of the media. At local level just about every town in the country has a press agency which survives on a diet of sports and court coverage as well as trying to sell 'local' stories into the regional and national outlets.

At national level, the biggest and most respected agency is called the Press Association (PA) and many organizations distribute their releases solely to PA. The advantage is that it is only one piece of paper, the disadvantage is that there is no guarantee that PA will decide to put your story out on its wire service. The other press agencies which you should be aware of are the National News Agency, which also feeds into the UK media, Reuters, Associated Press, and United Press International which are all international agencies. Distribution of your material to these last three can mean your story ending up literally anywhere in the world.

So the secrets of good distribution are:

- compile a comprehensive list of your local media and use it;
- don't re-invent the wheel – if your local university or research organization already has good lists and distribution systems, use them;
- at national level, think laterally about all the specialist correspondents and other outlets who might find your story useful;
- don't ignore any sector of the media – freelances, magazines, and press agencies all need your stories to survive.

Timing

You've got your release beautifully presented and you've decided who to send it to, but when should you send it? In news terms, 'news' happens today and tomorrow, not yesterday, so your release has got to reach its target audience in time for them to react.

Newspapers and magazines. Your decision making on timing will depend greatly on who you have chosen as your targets. If you just want to hit the monthly magazine sector then you have to understand how that sector works and the deadlines to which they work. The general interest monthlies are usually working at least two, and in some cases three, months ahead. The deadlines for the weekly mags and/or papers usually mean that no copy can be included after two or three days prior to publication day. For instance, the *Times Higher Education Supplement*'s deadline is usually Tuesday afternoon for Friday publication, so anything which arrives after that day will not go into that week's edition.

The daily papers need a minimum of 24 hours (unless it's a mega-story). This time is essential so that the journalist can convince the news editor that the story is worth writing; so that the writing can actually be done; and so that the editing process can be completed by the various daily deadlines that operate within the newspaper offices. (For more detail on newspaper deadlines see *Chapter 2*).

Radio. Radio news has the shortest lead time of all. It is possible for them to receive a media release in the morning post and for you and your story to appear on the lunch-time bulletins. However, again it is worth realizing that all stories have to be 'sold' up the managerial decision-making chain, so time needs to be built into the process to allow this to happen. Whilst radio news is very fast, radio features and magazine programmes usually need at least three to five days to decide, plan and act. These are usually weekly programmes and the planning for next week's show will start as soon as they have finished recording this week's.

Television. While television news may appear to be instant with satellite link-up to remote areas of conflict, this is only true for very major stories. TV has to have pictures, which means that the logistics of getting camera and sound equipment to wherever they are required has to be minutely planned; this takes time and a series of positive decisions. You must also realize that equipment is limited, and therefore TV is constantly having to make priority decisions. Sometimes these are not made on the editorial strength of a story but on logistical considerations such as: can we get a crew there, and is it an efficient use of resources? Because TV news is so expensive it is without doubt the most cost-conscious sector of the media.

TV programmes such as *Horizon* or *Antenna* can take months and months to prepare but this should not dissuade you from sending them your release. Your piece of paper may be just the prompt needed for a programme idea a year or so down the line. *Tomorrow's World* prides itself on being an up-to-the-minute magazine programme, but again they still need time to decide, plan and prepare the various items for the show. So don't expect them to be able to do much with and for you in less than a week or 10 days.

Freelancers. Freelance journalists work predominantly in the features area and they have to sell their ideas to the features or news desk before they can start work. This can take some time, so the freelance writer will always be pleased to receive your release as far in advance as possible.

So, having generally surveyed the scene and tried to point out some of the distinct deadline differences inherent within different sectors of the media, is there a general guideline about when we should send out our releases? Well, yes and no. No, in that there is no single best time to catch all sectors of the media. But yes, in terms of hitting a majority and especially hitting the news part of the media. For optimum results send your release out about 10 or 14 days before the event. This allows the specialist correspondent to evaluate your story, perhaps do some background research or talk to other experts. Both radio and TV can then enter your news event in their forward planning diaries and make decisions about allocating the necessary resources. This allows the freelance journalist to sell on your story into the features sections. This timing also allows you some time to follow-up your release by phoning a few of your key targets and asking them if they are going to cover your story.

Composition

So you've decided on what your release should look like, who you are going to send it to, and when you are going to send it out. Now all you have to do is write it. As was said earlier, good media release writing should ape a newspaper news story. The object of the exercise is to get your release to appear in print just as you wrote it. So, the first thing to say is: read newspapers; see what words they use; how they structure a story; and how long the average story is. This kind of basic research is essential if you are going to produce a usable release. Writing for the media is a totally different discipline than writing for science's usual audiences.

A media release is not a research report, nor a journal article, nor a conference abstract, nor a book chapter, nor a set of lecture notes. A media release is a self-contained story, told in 200–250 words, which contains 'the news' and an explanation of that news story.

The intro

When you read the news pages of your daily paper you'll quickly see that the intro, the first paragraph, always contains 'the news'. The object of this is that if the reader does no more than read the first paragraph of every single news story, then they will have got the news of the day. So, the intro is vital because it is the hook to get the reader to read on into the body of the story – a boring or irrelevant intro will guarantee your story is unread. The internal logic of the intro is that it must answer what is known in the journalistic trade, as the five 'Ws' – What?; Who?; When?; Where?; Why?. 'What?' = the news; 'Who?' = the person speaking, researching and their institutional affiliation; 'When?' = the time and day when the conference paper, research report is being given or published; 'Where?' = the place where the conference is taking place or the research has been done – if not a conference paper; 'Why?' = the explanation. Let's look at the following fictional intro:

WHAT?   A carrot extract can cure certain forms of cancer, Professor
WHO?   Joe Bloggs, from the Walsall Oncological Research Centre,
               told The British Cancer Research Society Conference
WHERE/WHEN? in London today, Friday 30 February.
WHY?   The carrot product, carrotozyn, works by cutting down and
               ultimately cutting off the supply of food to the cancer cells.

The rest of the release should build on this bald start and include such details as: what cancers does it cure and why?; how long has the research been going on?; is this an animal study or has it been tried out on humans?; can sufferers get better just by eating carrots – if not, how soon will the 'drug' be on the market?; how many people die each year from these cancers?; how long does it take for the cancer cells to die?; who funded the research?; why did you start looking at carrots?

Rules. Now we've seen how important it is to get the intro right, how can we ensure that our writing style is correct? There are a few basic rules for news writing, none of which are particularly difficult but, like all skills, you improve the more often you use them.

Rule number one is BE ACTIVE. By this we mean use the active rather than the passive voice in our writing. The news is all about people, things, events and interaction; news is about activity, and to bring these stories to life we have to use the active voice. Writing passively tends to be the normal scientific genre. Besides being dull and sometimes difficult to understand, it is nearly always long winded, and in a media release where every word is valuable the active voice is therefore a distinct advantage. Let's look at a couple of examples of the difference between passive and active writing:

Jones was arrested by the police – PASSIVE;
Police arrested Jones – ACTIVE (and shorter).

Seventy-three research participants were chosen by Professor Jones – PASSIVE;
Professor Jones chose seventy-three research participants – ACTIVE (and shorter).

A meeting will be held by the research committee next week – PASSIVE;

The research committee meets next week – ACTIVE (and shorter).

To write actively, the order of the elements of the sentence should be:

SUBJECT – VERB – OBJECT

Rule number two is BE POSITIVE. News is about things happening and people doing things, so our releases have to tell the audience what *did* happen rather than what *didn't* happen. The object of this rule is to eliminate the negatives from our writing. So whenever you are about to write 'not' re-write the sentence in a positive form. For instance:

The experiments were not successful – NEGATIVE.
The experiments failed – POSITIVE (and shorter).

The MRC say they will not proceed with their plans – NEGATIVE.
The MRC say they have dropped their plans – POSITIVE (and shorter).

The Ethics Committee did not pay attention to the complaint – NEGATIVE.
The Ethics Committee ignored the complaint – POSITIVE (and shorter).

You will again note that positive writing uses less words and as you only have one side of A4 available, anything which reduces the verbiage is an advantage.

Rule number three is BE CONCISE. Scientific writing is often very complex, with long sentences containing lots and lots of qualifying clauses, and introducing secondary concepts. This writing style is inappropriate for the media market.

Within the context of being concise, the simple concept to understand is that each sentence must be limited to one idea. Again, actually reading newspaper news stories will be a bonus, so that you can see and understand the way different types of sentence construction are used to make the story readable.

The English language has three different types of sentences – the 'simple', the 'compound' and the 'complex'. When you read the average newspaper you will find that very few complex sentences are used and that the most used sentence type is the 'simple', together with a judicious number of 'compound'.

Looking at some examples of the different kind of sentence construction will hopefully help to explain this:

Two people joined the department yesterday.
(Simple sentence: one subject, one statement.)

Two people joined the department yesterday and raised the total number of staff to 31.

(Compound sentence: this is really two simple sentences joined together, usually with the word 'and'.)

Two people, from the USA, joined the department yesterday, as a result of an advertising campaign, raising the total staff to 31.
(Complex sentence: it has one main statement, but one or more subordinate clauses.)

The newspapers' predominant use of the 'simple' and 'compound' sentence is no accident. They have, and continually do, research and monitor their readers to find out exactly what they can and cannot easily comprehend. Complex sentences, even when limited to a single idea, are inherently more difficult to read and take in information from than the other two types. The newspapers' aim is to ensure that every reader reads every article in every edition easily. If the reader stumbles over a difficult sentence construction then it is likely that they will stop and move elsewhere.

Banned words, phrases and jargon. Part of the media's constant research into comprehensibility is to look at words and phrases. Every newspaper has a 'style book', the in-house editorial rule book which every journalist must follow. The decisions about what words and phrases are and are not allowed, are based on two considerations.

First, is the word ambiguous; does it have two or three potential meanings depending on context? Second, can the word be understood by the reader; is it beyond their 'reading age'? Each newspaper knows the reading age of its readership very accurately. For the *Mirror, Sun, Star* it is seven, for the *Mail* and *Express* it is ten and for the qualities, *Times, Independent, Guardian* and so on, it is twelve.

Just some of these banned words and phrases appear in *Table 5.1*. They have all been taken from various newspaper style books. Some will perhaps surprise you, but all have better, clearer and unambiguous alternatives given in brackets.

Table 5.1. Banned words and phrases and their alternatives

---

accordingly (*so*)	in consequence of (*because*)
apparent (*clear, plain*)	in excess of (*more than*)
commence (*start, begin*)	initiate (*start*)

consult (*talk to, see, meet*)	necessitate (*need, require*)
discontinue, terminate (*stop, end*)	obtain, receive (*get*)
dwelling, residence (*home*)	regulation (*rule*)
economical (*cheap*)	state (*say*)
endeavour, attempt (*try*)	statutory (*legal, by law*)
erroneous (*wrong, false*)	supplementary (*extra, more*)
facilitate (*help*)	utilize (*use*)

Jargon is a problem for all professionals when they are communicating with the non-initiated. Jargon is an in-group shorthand which reinforces our bonds with our peer group, but is *verboten* for media releases. There are two ways to deal with jargon in release writing. The first (and preferred) way is to eliminate it totally by finding the plain english version, but sometimes this is impossible when dealing with technical terms. The second solution, particularly when dealing with these technical terms, is at the first usage of the jargon term, explain in brackets – even if this takes a sentence or two – exactly what the term means. After this explanation you are free to use your jargon term further on in your release. This may sound like a rather convoluted requirement, but you must remember that only a small minority of your target audience will understand the jargon words, and if we are to communicate effectively then jargon must be either eliminated or explained in detail.

• • •

Well-written and well-presented media releases are vital to the process of getting our stories/events/news to the public via the media. Some key points to note are:

The four keys to a successful release:
1. proper design;
2. effective distribution;
3. perfect timing;
4. correct composition.

The importance of 'correct composition':
1. it should ape the structure of a newspaper story;

2. news first, then explanations and subsidiary information;
3. '5 Ws' in first paragraph – What? Who? Why? When? Where? Answer all these questions.

Writing style – six points to note:

1. be active;
2. be positive (delete the negatives);
3. be concise – one idea per sentence;
4. avoid jargon;
5. use first names (as well as titles);
6. be accurate (check your facts).

And finally, write for your audience – the journalists and the public beyond, not your peers.

6 THE MEDIA INTERVIEW

The new rules □ Speaking to newspapers and magazines □ Interviews on radio and TV □ Phone interviews □ Everyday language □ Questions □ Visible means of support □ Practise!

In the majority of cases it is not an ordeal to be interviewed by a journalist/reporter/presenter/ from the media. However, if you have not given an interview before you may well envisage the experience as falling somewhere between a session with a ham-fisted dentist and a serious head-to-head during the Spanish Inquisition. If so, you are probably a victim of the 'I-Know-Someone-Who-Did-An-Interview-Once-and-It-Was-A-Nightmare' syndrome. Stories of (usually live) radio or television interrogations in which the interviewee was all but roasted alive are legion. So too are accounts of gross misrepresentations in the Press, of shocking travesties, even lies.

Leaving aside the folklore surrounding interviews, the facts are that:

- only a tiny fraction of interviewees feel dissatisfied;

- often these have reason to be not through other people's actions but through their own;

- reports of interviewee ordeals are usually greatly exaggerated by fourth and fifth hand retelling.

You have to remind yourself that being interviewed represents a genuine opportunity for you to display your knowledge, spread the word about your discipline, department or institution and build a bridge between the 'ivory tower' of research and the world at large. An opportunity, undoubtedly, though at the same time, a bit of a challenge. You are translocating yourself intellectually and often physically from your familiar domain to an alien environment. You suddenly find yourself playing by a different set of rules without knowing exactly where the goalposts have been put.

The New Rules

These are few in number and pretty basic.

1. This is a lay environment: the general idea is to help people understand your science or technology, not to update your peers or impress your superiors.
2. The general public does not want theory, technicality or complex niceties but results, implications and, if possible, applications that flow from your research.
3. The media knows exactly what it wants from you.
4. You have to put yourself in their hands.
5. At any stage you can say 'no', or pull out, or ask for further clarification of what is wanted from you.

Of these five, probably none is more important than number 4 – put yourself in the media's hands. If a journalist asks you an offbeat, tangential or what seems to be a slightly foolish question, answer it. He or she is trying to clarify something for a purpose, often asking questions he or she thinks the public would want to ask. For example, suppose you are a particle physicist and the interviewer asks whether your search for the fundamental, universal laws of Nature could end in your 'discovering' God. Do not resort to put downs such as 'Well, of course, science has nothing to do with religion' or 'Well, actually I don't think that's an especially useful question'.

It is not for you to tell another professional what his or her job is. Nor is it particularly helpful PR on your part to lecture someone on the differences between science and religion. Accept the question for what it is (with some exceptions which will be touched on later in this chapter) and try to give a helpful, friendly answer. A bit of diplomacy can work wonders for your media image – which is after all what we are discussing – how you project yourself and are perceived by the public at large.

It is helpful to both sides if scientists can see the interview as an opportunity for the journalist to elicit information in a form a lay audience will understand, rather than an adversarial contest of wills.

All of these points relate to being interviewed in general. Let us now look at the different demands made by the various branches of the media in more detail.

Speaking to Newspapers

There are three main ways in which scientists will experience newspaper interviews. These are:

- individual face-to-face interviews;

- telephone interviews; and

- press conferences.

Face-to-face

In face-to-face encounters, the print journalist will fix up an interview and turn up at your office or laboratory, or invite you to come in to the newspaper, to talk about your work.

Photographs. It's possible they may ask to bring a photographer along or ask if this can be done at another time, when they have a clearer idea of the story and have had a chance to assess the photographic potential of the location. Scientists are usually more shy of having their photo taken than they are of being interviewed, but for a big story a picture of some sort is necessary. It's easier to acquiesce with good grace than undergo a barrage of requests from an increasingly anxious picture editor.

Setting ground rules. Before starting the interview, you are quite within your rights to set out the ground rules and aims as you see them, and any terms which you feel need setting – for example, no confidential patient details to be divulged. Don't expect the journalist to be delighted if you set too many conditions. Ideally negotiation should be done at the setting-up stage. Trying to do it when the journalist is in the office in front of you with an open notebook will cause great irritation.

A likely scenario in which you might want to set conditions is when you have just published a report – or are known to be about to – and the reporter wants to find out more. If you are not prepared to talk about the exact details of your work, for fear of jeopardizing publication in a science journal, then say so clearly at the outset and not at the end when you both may have invested many hours of conversation.

Off the record. Unless you say something is 'off the record' then all you say is usually taken down for potential use. It is no good getting carried away, being massively indiscreet about a colleague's work and then saying, 'That's off the record.' The terms *have* to be agreed beforehand. But the surest way of not being quoted is not to say it. However, the vast majority of journalists do respect off the record conversations, provided they have been mutually agreed beforehand. The convention means the words will not be attributed or traceable to you, but the information is still usable.

If an insider will speak frankly about the true situation, it will guide the journalist in writing a more informed piece. Even if your comments have been off the record, the journalist is still free to go to other sources to try to get them to talk *on* the record about information you have supplied, for instance, on a looming budget deficit or the likely closure of a controversial unit.

Non-attributable conversations are the staple fare of politicians; the whole lobby system at the House of Commons revolves around this principle. Politicians subtly and not so subtly disparage the opposition, civil servants, and leak unpopular proposals to gauge public opinion or to soften up anger when the unpopular announcement is finally made. High powered academics adept at working the funding system are also good at this game. If a non-attributable conversation provides the press with a good story, they will usually go along with it even though they know they are being used.

The risk in asking for lobby rules is that journalists know they are being used, and are wary of people with an axe to grind, because they are rarely likely to reveal the whole picture. Shroud-waving doctors make headline news, but they may also be trying to protect their own vested interests. Is it really the patients who will be damaged if a top London hospital closes, or is it the consultant's privileged position?

Asking to go off the record can make journalists very suspicious about your motives. Although it provides information they might not otherwise get, an off the record conversation also ties their hands. Furthermore, anonymous sources in an article are not as convincing as quotes from named individuals.

In general then, off the record briefings are not a good idea, despite the fact that civil servants adore them. If you've got something to say, say it openly, or don't say it at all. If you *are* convinced that going off the record is the best way forward, make sure the journalist accepts this before you start. Of course, parts of conversations can be off the record, and the rest on the record. But make it clear which is which, and be certain the journalist understands and accepts this.

Answer the questions. It is best to let the journalist ask the questions rather than trying to anticipate them or trying to steer the conversation into areas you think are more newsworthy. By all means tell the reporter what you think is important and exciting, but don't be surprised if he or she thinks something else is far more interesting. You might want to talk about gene-splicing or gravitational waves, but the reporter may want to talk about your hobbies, your family, where you went to school and what your favourite holiday resort is. If the journalist has been told to write a piece about 'the person behind the news' these are exactly the questions he or she will be asking. You can either play ball or say no, but it is silly to waste time talking at cross-purposes.

Generally, however, the interview will be a straightforward, question-and-answer session about your work. 'Will you explain what it is you do, and what it is you have found?' may be the opening and crucial question. It may be all that is needed, if you are willing to talk, to produce hundreds, if not thousands, of words. Subsequent questions are usually for clarification or amplification of particular points.

Invariably, stress will be placed on the practical implications and you will be asked questions about the timescale involved – when can we expect to see it at the bedside? In the High Street? In everyday use? You will be asked to speculate, but you are allowed to make it clear that it is only speculation. Saying 'A lot more work needs to be done but, with luck and sufficient funding, we might see it in use within five years' doesn't commit you to too much, but will make the journalist's day.

Telephone interviews

A usual occurrence, for journalists, is the telephone interview. Indeed most print journalism is done on the telephone, rather than face-to-face, because of time and logistic problems in getting to people, and because journalists very rarely know from day to day what they might be doing or who they might need to talk to.

The scientist may receive a telephone call out of the blue, from someone they have probably never heard of, asking for help. A reporter may be trying to understand a piece of research or get a comment on something that has happened that day, or checking details. It's fairly routine for the journalist to check details of a journal article, say in *The Lancet* or *Nature*, with the authors, to make sure the facts have been understood and to get some lay explanations and quotes to humanize the science.

In such cases at least the scientist is familiar with the work. Although you may not be the first author, or internal politics dictate that the reporter should talk to the professor rather than you, unless you know these people are contactable then and there, don't pass the reporter on. If you want to be humble about your own role in the research, fine. But the hard-pressed journalist might simply want some jargon translated into English and you are quite capable of doing this.

If you are busy or in the middle of a meeting it is perfectly acceptable to say that you can't talk now, but will be free in thirty minutes or an hour. Ask for a quick list of the questions the journalist wants answered and say you'll get back to him or her. If you give this undertaking, you must honour it.

Sometimes the call will not be about your work but someone else's, asking for a reaction, an explanation because the author is not available, or for it to be put in context. A new report saying an acid in fish oil can reverse certain types of solid tumour may provoke calls to a number of leading oncologists to ask if they've heard of this work and if it is likely to be helpful.

Similarly, 'scare' stories, such as the pill causing breast cancer, or cholesterol-lowering drugs causing people to commit suicide, are usually turned into 'Don't Panic' stories by responsible journalists who try to get mainstream scientists to put the controversial findings into perspective.

Other reports occasioning phone calls may have come from overseas and the news editor wants the British angle – are we doing anything along the same lines? Charlie Wilson, the acerbic former editor of *The Times*, epitomized this habit by spotting science stories from overseas on the agency wires and barking at his medical and science correspondents: 'Wrap a Union Jack around this.'

To speak or not to speak? Faced with the telephone call out of the blue, if you don't want to comment, then don't. But if you know someone else in the field who might feel more comfortable, then give the journalist that person's name and phone number.

If a reporter or specialist has been told to get some reaction to a story, he or she will doggedly pursue reaction. The danger in not responding is that the journalist will trawl through figures of ever-decreasing scientific repute, ending with the rent-a-quote candidate out of desperation. The idea to bear in mind is that if you don't comment, the chances are that it will be someone *less* well-qualified who will do so, rather than someone *more* qualified. Your reticence, however well-meaning, doesn't help genuine attempts to understand science.

Sometimes the phone call will be unrelated to any journal article but may have been prompted by a news event that day in your area of interest. A plane crash may spark a call to an occupational psychologists or ergonomist asking about the interface between people and complex machinery. A policewoman being stabbed in the heart, but surviving, may prompt questions to chest physicians or accident and emergency surgeons about the amount of damage the body can sustain and still recover.

With these type of calls, no great scientific knowledge or leading edge research is required; the reporter simply wants background information to make the story more understandable to readers. This is sometimes known in journalism as 'A doctor writes', after the *Private Eye* spoof. It means there will be five or six paragraphs at the side, or at the end, of a major story, often put in a separate box, giving the basic facts about a disease or scientific process. This will be straightforward, factual information, put in a readable way. What is plutonium? How many pints of blood are there in the body? What is reverse osmosis? You, as a scientist, might think that giving this information is demeaning or a waste of your time. But it is a great help to the journalist, who often hasn't got an exhaustive supply of reference books from which to cull such data.

Will you be quoted by name? It is not uncommon for reporters to spend 20 or 30 minutes talking to a scientist, and then to hear the scientist say at the end: 'You're not going to use any of this are you?' The reporter has not been ringing to pass the time of day! Unless the journalist says 'This is strictly for background. I won't quote you by name' then you will be quoted, and your name used, because it gives the piece authority. It is far more impressive that Professor Jack Bloggs of the University of London thinks the new report is flawed, than an unnamed spokesperson. The rule is that if you talk to a journalist, you will almost certainly be quoted. If you don't want your name used, you must stress this. Even so, the words may still appear, under the guise of 'a leading expert said last night . . .'.

Is there a hidden agenda? Some scientists seem paranoid that journalists have some sort of hidden agenda and want to make fools of them or incriminate them in some way. In 99.9% of cases this is rubbish. However, it does pay to know where the journalist is from and what type of article he or she has in mind.

So called 'investigative' journalists do often set out with a premise and then try to find the data to fit it. If someone is from *Panorama* or *The Sunday Times Insight* team they are going to be more interested in 'doing a number' on someone than the normal medical or science correspondent. If you're approached by such a journalist, it pays to be careful. If they are exposing a crook, and want your help or comment in doing so, this may be entirely laudable, but when the libel writs fly you'll be in the firing line too.

Some journalists thrive on promoting scientific mavericks and making the rest of the scientific community look like reactionary stick-in-the-muds. People who believe HIV does not cause AIDS, or that cholesterol is not damaging to the heart, are of far more interest to such journalists than the thousands of researchers who do not share these views.

If you are asked to take part in such interviews try to ascertain the purpose and aims of the article beforehand. If you do take part or agree to be interviewed, and you have your own tape recorder, tape the conversation yourself so you have a certain record of what you said. Say that you are doing this, as telling journalists you are recording the conversation has a salutary effect on any liberties they may feel they can take with the copy.

Don't be drawn into areas of criticism that may have legal ramifications, unless you really feel strongly that something is a scandal or a particular practitioner is a charlatan and you are prepared for the possible consequences. When you're in the libel trial dock it's a bit late to say you wished the journalist hadn't used those comments.

No comment. Avoiding unwanted questions is an art in itself but, as any politician demonstrates, it is a fairly easily learned skill.

'That's an interesting question – but could I first just say', followed by five minutes of your views will deflect most unwanted questions. Really persistent journalists will repeat the question, probably four or five times in different ways, but 'I don't think that is the issue,' or 'I really haven't come here today to talk about that – the really important issue is . . .' can hold them at bay.

The thing NOT to say is 'No comment'. This immediately makes you look guilty, shifty, devious and as if you are trying to hide something. It will provoke far more questions than it will prevent.

If something has gone wrong, or reflects badly on yourself or your institution, the temptation to clam up is overwhelming. But in these cases saying more, rather than less, is usually the best course. Explain what happened, and put your side of the story; unless you do so, your case will go by default and only your critics will be heard. When a patient was shot in the middle of a busy London hospital the doctors who treated the man did not initially realize he was suffering from gunshot wounds. This provoked howls of ridicule from the press about incompetent surgeons. It was only when a surgeon started talking about the nature of gun-shot wounds and how these could be disguised by other injuries, as had happened in this case, that the story became less interesting.

A 'no comment' approach would have perpetuated the myth that doctors at that hospital were incompetent, whereas address-ing the events head on and providing a full description of the problems helped defuse the incident.

Unless there are overriding legal reasons why you cannot comment, then 'No comment' should only be used as the very last resort.

Can you see the copy beforehand? Following an interview you may ask, not unreasonably, if you can see the copy before it is used. 'No,' is the usual answer. Some newspapers have written rules about not showing copy to interviewees, in case it compro-mises the objectivity of the journalists. Daily news journalists have no time to send copy for approval, despite fax machines, even if they had the inclination to do so. The best you can hope for, if you are very lucky, is that the reporter will read over the copy to you on the phone. This will be done as a personal favour to you, and you cannot insist on it. If the interview is important enough, or you are important enough, a compromise can sometimes be reached and your quotes read to you, but not the whole article.

If you get this far, don't be pompous about the writing style, thinking you could write a better news story. But if something is wrong, say so. The journalist will usually instantly correct errors of fact, and may be prepared to tone down questions of interpretation. However, if it's clear you are simply backtracking because you've got cold feet about the things you said, that's just tough. There won't be changes on that basis.

By all means ask if you can have the copy read to you, but don't be at all surprised if the answer is 'no.' Such rules may sound harsh, but that is how the real world of journalism operates.

Press conferences

The third interview situation is the press conference. Some people find these something of an ordeal because they can be faced by massed ranks of vocal and demanding reporters and a phalanx of cameras and microphones.

On the other hand, there is usually a panel of scientists who can deal with various aspects of the issue rather than one person having to answer all the questions. The chairperson can deflect or head off irrelevant or improper questions, and also call an end to the proceedings. The press conference will usually begin with brief statements from the researchers, summing up the main points as they see them. Then the questions will begin. The guiding rule for press conferences is to answer the questions as clearly and as interestingly as you can, and try to enjoy the experience.

The first one or two questions are often the big important ones; journalists like to get these out of the way first in case time is pressing. Subsequent questions will be more detailed in order to tease out additional facts or put the research in context. Lots of questions don't mean you haven't been clear in your presentation, although this is sometimes the case. It usually means the journalists are interested. Far more embarrassing are press conferences when journalists have been left so stupefied, or bored, that there are no questions.

Unless you are asked for an incredible amount of scientific detail, say by the correspondent from *Nature*, then try to keep the answers on a level that will be understood by a lay audience. It's perfectly permissible to tell the specialized reporter that you will speak to them privately after the meeting rather than boring everyone else with arcane details.

At the end of the press conference, particularly interested

journalists will come forward to ask a few follow-up questions, or to make sure the spelling of your name is correct. There may also be requests for one-to-one interviews by radio and TV journalists, and it's a good idea to ask the organizers of the press conference beforehand if there is a quiet room you can use for interviews, rather than having to rush around at the last minute or stand in corridors.

By definition, a press conference has been called to give something publicity, so it helps to be enthusiastic rather than defensive or over-cautious. You may find the whole process stimulating, and having to respond to lay questions may help clarify previously unarticulated thoughts about the purpose of the research.

Being interviewed is a bit like skiing – it seems scary at first but once you get over your nerves it can be great fun. Relax! Enjoy it and you'll come across far more impressively than if you appear cautious and wooden.

Speaking to Magazines

Journalists who ring you from magazines will mostly be freelances; occasionally they may be on staff. Usually the editor or features editor will have had what they think is a brilliant idea in the bath, and sent some poor hapless soul out to do the piece. This will be regardless of whether there is any relevant research (they won't know that) and regardless of how controversial it is (they won't know that either). Unlike newspapers, magazines are mostly filled with long pieces or features rather than news-orientated, short items. You are more likely to be asked general questions about an area than to comment on a specific incident.

Communicating on an area not your own

Being asked about a particular event may, however, sometimes happen. Scientists are (understandably) not always terribly comfortable with this unless they feel very knowledgeable about the incident and confident about the relevant interpretations. Although you have every right to refuse to comment, of course, such current events can provide excellent 'pegs' for getting sound science across to the public. One way of dealing with it is to say that you don't want to discuss that specific incident, but you will talk about the *general* issues.

You may not know exactly why there was a leak at a British

nuclear reactor, for example, but you may be able to talk about nuclear safety at a broader level. Again, it is widely regarded as unethical for a professional to make comments about a particular individual to the media. So what can you do (other than saying 'no, sorry') if a journalist wants a comment on, say, the Chancellor of the Exchequer going bungee-jumping? You don't have to say that you always thought the guy had a death wish (unless you want to, of course), but you *can* discuss research on the pressures of high office, or evidence that financially-orientated men score highly on measures of sensation-seeking. These are points that the journalist can weave into the feature without you having to do a specific analysis of a particular person or incident.

Quotes

Magazine journalists do like facts and data if they exist. If they don't, or are not exactly in the form that's required, then journalists can still survive as long as they can get quotes. For them, quotes from a scientist *are* data. In fact, scientists can sometimes be surprised that their interview takes up so much of a magazine article, and wonder why they didn't write it themselves.

If asked for quotes in an area in which there is directly relevant research, it is relatively straightforward. You can describe your own research, and perfectly legitimately that of others. For example, 'Experiments have shown that mice born within a 100-mile radius of Chernobyl are faintly luminescent'; 'Research finds that 15% of marriages hit the rocks in the first year.' The purpose is to get good science across to the public, and it is not necessary for you personally to have done the experiments before you're prepared to talk about them.

Sometimes you may know of no directly relevant research, and it is vital to say so. Make clear that this doesn't mean there isn't any (unless you're certain of this) as you don't want to curtail the journalist's search prematurely. But you may still be able to help. You may know of some peripherally relevant research, and the journalist may (or may not) be able to make some use of this. Due to their pressing need to write 2,000 words on this topic which they know nothing (or little) about, they will probably be deeply grateful for any interesting snippet.

It may also be possible for you to make informed guesses on the basis of what you do know:

'No, we haven't taken samples of Pluto's surface, but our knowledge of

planet formation does make it extremely unlikely that it's made of crushed diamonds.'

'I know of no studies on whether individuals with large phone bills are happier. But given what we know about how social support can relieve the effects of stress, and having friends is good for our physical health, it's likely that a call a day keeps the doctor at bay.'

Have confidence that your accumulated knowledge is worth something and that journalists want it. The job of magazine journalists, like any others, is to produce an article that is interesting, a 'good read', targeted at their particular audience and as accurate as possible.

Accuracy

Scientists who have had a bad experience with the press, for whatever reason, tend to form the opinion that accuracy doesn't matter to journalists as long as the story sounds exciting. The odd widely-discussed 'horror story' can spread alarm and despondency even further into the scientific community. But with rare exceptions, the idea that journalists don't care about accuracy is untrue. Inaccuracies are most likely to creep in because a complicated matter has not been explained sufficiently clearly, or a sub-editor has sharpened or tried to clarify the journalist's prose and in the process altered the sense (subs are not supposed to change meaning, but it can happen).

Despite what scientists may fear, it does journalists no good at all in terms of their reputation or in the eyes of their bosses if they get things wrong and incur complaints from interviewees or the public. However, in order to make the prose flow, they will almost certainly feel free to edit the quotes slightly as long as the sense remains intact.

Magazine journalists usually have longer to prepare their features than newspaper journalists, and may have less investment in making all the quotes fit a particular angle. Having said that, they usually have ideas of their own which they would like you to endorse. 'But hormone replacement therapy really is the answer to conquering ageing for women, isn't it?'; 'Keeping the bedroom light on all night will help people beat Seasonal Affective Disorder, won't it?'; 'Cellular telephones can damage your health, can't they?' It's very important not to let any sympathy for their predicament (an editor with his/her own views breathing down the journalist's neck) and enthusiasm (for their own ideas) colour what you say. In normal conversation, we often say social-wheels-oiling things like 'Uh huh, but I actually think . . .' or 'Yes, but . . .' This can be a big mistake. Depending on the journalist's desperation/ lack of scruples, such politeness may be interpreted as agreement with what they've said, and their views will go down in quotes with your name attached. So just say straightforwardly, 'I'm afraid there's no evidence for that at all,' or 'I think that's very unlikely', or some other very clear refutation of the point. Then tell them what you think *is* the case.

Brevity

We have already discussed the need to avoid jargon, to be clear, to keep it simple, to avoid complications and ambiguities, to give concrete examples where possible (from real life and/or research) and so on. It is important to keep each answer short if you can, as the longer and more complicated your answer, the greater the likelihood of the journalist getting it a bit wrong or editing the quote (probably inadvertently) in a misleading way. It is also the case that, as with newspaper interviews, the most vivid phrases are the most likely to be used. In the long 'informed guesses' examples given, the two sentences that will certainly survive the editing process are 'It's extremely unlikely that it's made of crushed diamonds', and 'A call a day keeps the doctor at bay'. Vivid imagery grabs the attention and stays in the memory. Journalists' eyes light up when they hear it.

One of us gave an interview to the *The Sunday Times* on the publication of Alex Comfort's *The New Joy of Sex*. The journalist described the book's revisions in the light of AIDS, and the interviewee's immediate response was 'Goodness, it should be called *The New Joys of Celibacy*', before proceeding to give a long and careful interview about the psychological issues raised by the advent of the disease. And what was the one quote that appeared on the front page of the paper? You guessed it. The joke.

Checking quotes

Magazines, however, will usually give more space to your quotes than newspapers will. But it is still the case that the precise choice of quotes is up to the journalist, who will select them once all the material is collected and an angle (if not determined initially) and structure decided on. As with newspapers, it is not normal practice to check quotes with interviewees. You have the right to ask, and they may or may not agree. Time pressures or magazine policy or feelings that they are being 'monitored' may prevent them; but this is not always the case and they may be willing. You can also tell them that if they want to check anything with you, to please do so. This means that if they have points they need clarifying, checking or elaborating they know they can, which may be good for the accuracy of the final product.

You can assume that *anything* you say is fair game to be quoted unless it has been agreed beforehand that it is 'off the record' (for more on this see p. 92). So it is important not to get carried away, which can happen when you are deeply involved in an interview on a topic you feel passionate about with a very socially skilled journalist. If you do accidentally say something like 'Yes, I feel sure that a cure for AIDS is in sight', your only hope is to plead and beg for them not to quote that. As it is probably the most thrilling thing you've said in the whole interview, this will be very upsetting for the journalist indeed. Saying juicy things and then retracting them or saying 'that's off the record' raises their blood pressure, but if they are kind, they will let you off.

The time at which you are in greatest danger of blurting out regrettable things actually comes at the end of the interview, when you're in the process of saying goodbye and you're feeling off guard – and the journalist asks one last question or a thought springs to mind. But forewarned is forearmed.

One last thing. Before they go, check that they have your title and job description correctly, and have spelt your name right.

Interviews on Radio and Television

Setting the agenda

If a broadcaster approaches you for an interview or any other kind of contribution to a programme it is essential to establish at the outset exactly what it is that is wanted of you, if you are to avoid conflict, disappointment, frustration or under-achievement. To avoid this ask a series of searching questions:

- What is the programme on which I'll be appearing? (What is the type of audience; level of their understanding; is the format magazine or documentary?)

- What questions do you want to discuss? (This is not so much the actual questions but the areas to be covered.)

- Is the programme live or pre-recorded?

- Will I be appearing solo or as part of a group? If the latter, who else is scheduled to appear?

- How long an interview do you want? And where do you want to do it? (You may for example feel happier if the interviewer meets you on your own ground with a portable recorder rather than face a proper studio.)

- How much will I be paid? (That too depends on how much disruption to your working day the interview might entail.)

If you do not get clear-cut replies to any or all of these questions, or you do not feel confident in the person to whom you are talking – the producer, researcher, presenter or reporter – then you are not obliged to co-operate. Many interviews have floundered because both parties had not spelt out beforehand what they wanted or hoped for.

It is vital to establish the agenda *before* the interview. During the interview is not the time to discuss ground rules. Indeed the more notice you have of what is required the better able you will be to deliver the goods. Try to establish the agenda without sounding too inflexible or pompous. Ask in a fact-finding spirit, not in a surly mood of defensiveness. Part of the agenda, as we have said, concerns the level of comprehension of the audience. Here it pays to ask in advance whether listeners are likely to understand your terminology. If not, you have time to work out some simplified alternatives; far better than having to improvise on the spot during the interview itself. Many broadcasters like to have such preliminary discussions, it gives them confidence too that the scientist they are talking to has some media professionalism.

'I'm no good at that sort of thing'

Do not be unduly modest; you are probably a much better radio and television interviewee than you think you are. The reason why you may have reservations about your abilities is perhaps that you have not thought sufficiently about what 'that sort of thing' really is.

A successful broadcast interview is not a virtuoso performance by either or both of the two players but an interesting conversation that the audience feels it has overheard. Indeed some of the best radio and television of all times has occurred when interviewers and interviewees have appeared to forget where they were and simply talk – disjointedly sometimes, but always with the elements of good conversation: humour; enthusiasm; knowledge; speculation.

In other words, do not disqualify yourself from taking part in radio and television because you feel you are not sufficiently extroverted or histrionic or articulate or downright conceited to make public your research. A friendly, quiet tone makes a better impression than a know-all professional one. Enthusiasm catches the attention more readily than ringing but empty displays of erudition. In short, you can succeed as a broadcaster simply by being yourself.

Finding your 'voice'. It may take a little time, of course, to find your particular self or 'voice'. Some of the best broadcasters you can think of were fairly inept performers when they started, but hit the mark when they began to find a personal style with which they felt comfortable. Indeed, comfort is really your objective. You are trying to reach a state of easy, relaxed talking that represents you and no one else. That takes a bit of practice. But even if you never reach that blissful goal of self-satisfaction, just doing a few practice interviews with friends and colleagues will produce quite dramatic improvements.

You do not even need someone else to interview you – interview yourself, in your head. Role-play interviewer and interviewee. Think critically about what sounds better; will a listener prefer 'The results, from a statistical point of view, were unequivocal' or 'Frankly, the results hit you between the eyes'.You will find that you will improve quite dramatically with such exercises.

Disembodied Voices: the 'Line' Interview

Not all interviews are conducted face-to-face. For reasons of logistics or time pressure it may be suggested that you go to a local radio or TV studio which is linked by line to another where the interviewer is located. It can be a slightly daunting experience to hear a voice in your headphones talking to you as if in person and to be expected to respond in similar fashion. There are no non-verbal cues, no signs from the interviewer that he or she wants to intervene or indications from you that you are coming to the end of your point. In fact, for this very reason, interviewees who are not used to lines tend to go on a bit too long with their replies, and may also sound impersonal and declamatory.

The trick is to think of it as a telephone conversation. Instead of talking blindly into the ether, imagine that you are talking intimately to one person, pausing, asking for comment perhaps. This makes for a genuine two-way communication.

In all other aspects though, the line interview is no different from any other. You should still set an agreed agenda; discuss areas to be covered and avoided; sit fairly still and keep the pace of your voice even. Don't try to mask the loneliness by gabbling.

'Talk low, talk slow and don't move around too much'

It was the late John Wayne – Hollywood cowboy extraordinaire – who coined the above advice to the young film actor. It might well be worth remembering this during the broadcast interview itself.

Anxiety, nervousness, and inexperience tend to make people talk too quickly. Often when they do, the voice goes up in pitch so that what should have been a measured stream of fascinating research comes out as falsetto machine gun fire.

Nervousness and unfamiliarity with the technical trappings of a studio can often generate too much body movement. Typically, an interviewee may be sitting down chatting to the interviewer before the recording or live programme begins. A studio technician asks the interviewee to say a few words for level (no, not always 'What did you have for breakfast?' because at 8 p.m., it is usually impossible to remember). Once satisfied with the positioning and balancing of the microphones, he tells the producer all is ready. The interview begins. Question one: 'So tell me a bit about the background of your recent study?' At this point the interviewee looks reflective, sits back in the chair, looks to the ceiling and says something that is barely audible. Or, he replies 'I'm glad you asked me that', leans forward intently, thumps the table with his elbow, drums out a percussion exercise with his fingers and totally ruins his answer by thunderous noises off.

Keep still. Sit in a comfortable position while the level is being taken, perhaps resting on your elbows, hands crossed on the table. Once the interview begins, stay there! In fact with practice, you will find that you are able to gesticulate if you wish while maintaining a fixed distance from the microphone. But as a novice try to keep stationary.

Keep your delivery fairly deliberate. It may seem slow to you, but for a radio audience in particular, hearing what you have to say once and once only, it will be perfectly acceptable. There is nothing more frustrating to the listener than missing a key point because an interviewee was in full gallop.

Everyday Language: Forget the Grammar Book and the Jargon

Many interviewees, especially first-timers, are anxious to 'talk proper'. Now this is a little odd; in everyday speech few of us talk with measured, grammatical correctness, each subordinate clause perfectly articulated with the next to produce a balanced Ciceronian sentence. Quite the contrary. We stop, start, double back, repeat, 'um' and 'er', slip in asides, jokes, tail off and pick up somewhere else. Just listen to any conversation around you.

Now, although too much disjointedness can become tiresome and confusing, the naturalness of everyday conversation is what you should be aiming for. This is, after all, a *conversation* not a monologue. A good interviewer will ask the sort of questions he or she feels the person in the street might ask; your job is to reply in the everyday terms that anyone can understand.

Some tips on interview 'language'

- Make no assumptions about the expectations of your listeners other than that they want to hear something interesting and enthusiastic.

- Do not try to create beautiful sentences or play a role that is not you. Be yourself. Use your own turns of phrase.

- If you can find a reasonable joke as you go along, crack it.

- Above all, discard jargon. This is particularly important in radio and television where, as we have said, you are talking in real time. Unlike a book or magazine article, a broadcast programme is ephemeral. The listener has to get it first time. So, to say that a result is 'statistically significant' or that someone's cells are 'morphologically undifferentiated' or that behaviour is 'neurophysiologically determined' or that 'CERN researchers are looking for the Higgs boson' puts considerable demands on listeners who may well be hearing a word or phrase for the first time.

The jargon of your trade is so familiar to you that it has ceased to be jargon at all – in your view. Not so the average listener. If you can, put your ideas into plain english. If you feel that there is a particular technical phrase that you simply must use, then use it but have an explanation to tack on to it. Do not hope that this explanation will come out of the blue while you are speaking: work it out beforehand so that it is familiar to you. As an exercise, why not pick five or six phrases from your area of research and try putting them into everyday language. Try them out on someone who is not in your field of research, or not in research at all, such as the man on the bus or, as the Americans so graphically put it, 'Joe Sixpack'.

Questions, Questions

Unless you want to avoid a topic (see the following section on deflection), then answer the question put to you. That means listening to what the questioner says. This may sound fairly self-evident, but a surprising number of interviewees tend to answer questions of their own making, sticking to a rigid formula they have in their heads instead of remaining flexible and responsive.

What usually happens is something like this. You agree a series of questions with the interviewer, who duly asks you numbers 1, 2 and 3. Then, halfway through your reply to number 3, the reporter's imagination/memory/news sense is caught by one of your passing phrases. So instead of moving on in pre-ordained fashion to question 4, the interviewer slips in 3b, 3c and even 3d. Let him or her do this. Don't ignore the detour and answer a question that was never asked. The interviewer will come back to number 4 in due course. And if he or she does not, it is not the end of the world, is it?

Deflection

Sometimes, in spite of all the preparation you have done to make sure the interview goes the way you want it to, you may get asked an awkward question. You came to the studio prepared to talk about particle physics but after a few questions on quarks and neutrinos you are asked point blank 'Are you in favour of nuclear energy?' Or you have just finished a brilliant account of your excellent research when the interviewer says 'Isn't this all just common sense, though?'

At this point you have to curb your understandable immediate desire to reach across and tweak his bow tie. It is *never* productive to get angry or to try to belittle the interviewer. Often the person asking the questions is something of a national or local celebrity – a wellknown presenter for a local radio station, for example. You risk alienating your audience immediately if you reply 'What kind of smartypants question is that, mate?'

Cultivate the art of graceful deflection. If you do not like a question, answer: 'I'm glad you asked me that. It's a very important point and I'd like to come back to it in a moment. For now though, just let me say . . .'. And you go on to say what you wanted to anyway, without losing face or the audience.

There are variations on this, namely:

'That's a good question. Another one, related to it, is . . .'.

'Well, before we get on to that, can I just give you a bit of background . . .'.

There is of course an alternative, more direct strategy. You can come clean and say 'I'm sorry, I don't know' or 'That's not really my area/field/specialism.' Or even 'Search me!' Humility can sometimes be very refreshing and empathic.

Visible Means of Support

Almost every interview on research will involve statistics. Part of your preparation for a media interview should be a brief (150 words at most) résumé of the chief numerical points. For example, you might draw up something like this:

CARROT EATING AND MEMORY

- 100 people, 50 male/50 female

- 10 lbs of carrots a week for 6 weeks

- 12% improvement on memory test

● Further studies on potatoes, pineapples, grapes next year

CONTACT: I.M. Müncher 0882 739 761

Such an *aide-mémoire* serves several functions. For one thing, you can keep it in front of you during a radio interview to make sure you get your facts right. There is nothing more irritating for a broadcaster than to get a telephone call the day after an interview along the lines of 'Sorry, but you know I said there was a 24% memory improvement, well I should have said 12% – I was getting mixed up with an earlier study'. At least get your facts straight yourself.

Second, after the interview, leave the data with the producer as a cue sheet. If your interview is cut down, the presenter may need a few facts for a script which have inadvertently been thrown away on the edited tape. Include on it too your name and contact number in case at the last minute you need to be asked to clarify something.

The fact sheet can also include a simple graphic such as a graph, pie chart or Venn diagram. It could, if appropriate, contain a colourful little fact such as the best known carrot-lover in history or some of the most remarkable memory feats on record. Material such as this, provided it is pithy and short, can be invaluable to a programme-maker.

The good, the bad and the normal

Listen carefully to the radio and watch television with a view to judging the competence of interviewees on factual matters. You will find considerable variation, from the inept to the brilliant, with the majority falling somewhere in between.

You will find that media 'naturals' – those who are in command of themselves, their subject, the situation – are quite rare, at least the first time they try their hand. Even the apparently artless and effortless interviewee has probably improved with practice and growing confidence, often by self-consciously analysing his or her performances and making an effort to improve them.

There is a general lesson for everyone here. Excruciatingly bad interviewees are in truth pretty rare too, and like their more gifted counterparts, they too improve immensely with practice. In other words, wherever you seem to sit on the competence spectrum, you can always move upwards. People with no experience of the media who attend short media training courses – of one or even half a day – usually come away immeasurably better at answering questions than they were when they started the course. There is nothing like having a go; even a simulated interview pays off when you are faced with the real thing.

Practise!

Everyone can improve as an interviewee with practice. What is more, you can practise *outside* the radio or television studio. Here's how.

Try interviewing yourself in your head. Ask the sort of questions you think appropriate and then role-play the answers. Since a major hurdle for all science interviewees is the technicality of their subject, deliberately choose some tricky topics. How about 'What is a base pair?'; 'Can you explain electron spin resonance?'; or even 'How are we to visualize the concept of infinity?'

Try concocting alternative explanations. Try imagery (see *Concepts and Conceits* in *Chapter 4*). Try unpacking your research step-by-step. At first you will probably be a bit long-winded but you will soon arrive at a lively narrative.

Alternatively, find someone who is totally unfamiliar with your research area – perhaps a researcher from a different department, or his or her secretary – to ask you questions. Instruct the interviewer not to feign wisdom but to get you to explain everything and anything you say which is at all obscure.

If you really want to learn to communicate to the media, you can be a mock interviewee at any time – driving the car, in the bath, on a bus ride. Like an actor you can think yourself into the unfamiliar role of media expert, though of course the lines you speak will be your own.

Increasingly organizations such as universities and research institutions are tuning in to the practicalities of running media courses for their research personnel. Some will have their own radio and television production facilities and trained staff to run them. Avail yourself of these opportunities if they exist. If they do not, look outside for media training courses offered by private and academic organizations.

Debriefing

If you really disliked giving an interview or taking part in a phone-in, do not be too hasty in saying 'Never again!'. Try checking back with the producer a couple of days afterwards. He or she may be a lot more complimentary about your performance than you expected.

If you enjoyed the interview you could still call to get feedback and perhaps extend your broadcasting experience by offering to do more of the same or even to move into more demanding areas.

Talk too about your media experience with colleagues who have also been through it all. You may glean some useful tips – and vice versa.

A Media Training Course

Much of what has been written in this book so far could, and I'm sure will, be used within the context of media training events. There is no doubt that our ability to communicate with the media will enhance their treatment of our work as scientists. Therefore, the need for media training for our 'profession' is paramount.

This *Appendix* lays out in some detail a day's media training course. It is modelled on a format that The British Psychological Society has been using for some years, and which has been taken up by various other scientific organizations. The day is designed to be intensive and participative for a maximum of 16 persons. At the end of the day the 'students' should:

- understand how different parts of the media operate;
- understand how news writing differs from normal scientific communication;
- understand how to put together and distribute a media release; and
- understand how a media interview operates.

If, having read what follows, you have any queries on media training, any of the authors of this book would be only too happy to advise.

PROGRAMME

Session 1	10.00 a.m.	Course and Tutors/Participants Introduction
Session 2	10.20 a.m.	Press Conference/News Writing Exercise
Session 3	11.20 a.m.	Snapshots of the Media – National Newspapers – National and Local Radio – Magazines
Session 4	12.15 p.m.	Media Releases: Why and How?
	1.00 p.m.	Lunch

Session 5	1.30 p.m.	Media Release Writing Exercise
Session 6	2.30 p.m.	Being Interviewed by a Journalist
Session 7	4.30 p.m.	Review of the Media Release Exercise
Session 8	5.00 p.m.'ish	Course Round-up and Close

REQUIREMENTS

- You'll need a reasonably quiet room which can comfortably seat, boardroom style, all your 'students' and tutors.
- An OHP (overhead projector) and flipchart.
- Tea/coffee on arrival, a lunch of some description. (Don't make it too heavy or alcoholic, or the post-lunch sessions will suffer.) Tea/coffee for the afternoon break.
- Place name-cards or badges for all participants.
- Ask 'students' to bring pens/pencils and paper with them.
- Choice of tutors: it is always advisable to get in professional journalists (the best you can afford) to do the great majority of the work. Hearing the information from the 'professionals' tends to reinforce what is said and tends to be believed.

You'll see that the programme calls for three or four tutors – one generalist; one from radio; one from newspapers and one from magazines. (TV has been deliberately left out for two reasons: 1) to train someone properly in TV techniques takes a lot of expensive and intensive time; 2) at this level most scientists are more likely to interact with print and radio than with TV.)

Experience has shown that most journalists working in our field make quite good tutors as long as they are well briefed. Tell them exactly what you want them to do, or you may simply hear a series of anecdotes. This may be fascinating, but it is hardly the point of the exercise.

- Ensure that you have all the materials you require in sufficient quantities.
- Ensure that programmes and all back-up materials, such as copies of this book, are available for giving out either during or at the end of the course.
- Be very well-prepared and get to the venue in good time to meet the early-arriving participant – there's always one.

DETAILED NOTES ON THE PROGRAMME

All the paragraph numbers which follow refer to the session numbers on the programme. These notes are designed as an explanation for the course organizer and tutors and **should not be given to the students**.

1. Tutors/Participants Introduction

First introduce yourself and the tutors. Briefly explain the aims and objects of the course. Explain that the course is for the students' benefit and encourage them to participate as and when they want to.

Next, get the students to introduce themselves – name, job, why they've come on the course, what they hope to get out of it and any particular issues they would like to see covered (this last point can allow the tutors either formally or informally to take up individuals' particular concerns).

This shouldn't take longer than 10–15 minutes. The aim is to provide all those present with basic information and remind people what to expect.

2. Press Conference/News Writing Exercise

In this session each student plays the role of a news journalist. They attend a 'press conference', interview, en masse, the 'celebrity', and then write up a 200-word news story based on the interview. This session has several aims and objects:

- to stop the participants from being physicists, social workers or media researchers and enable them to think 'journalist/ communicator' as early as possible in the course;
- to show that news writing is a particular discipline demanding particular skills on the part of the writer;
- to show that deadlines and space constraints are the daily stuff of journalism;
- to show that detailed knowledge of the subject matter is not a vital component for the news writer; and
- to show that as long as a few simple rules are followed then the skills of news writing can be achieved. This last point is the real key.

So what do you say to the students? What is the brief?:

'For the next hour or so you are going to be news journalists. You are

going to attend a press conference, interview a famous scientist and write up the story in 200 words.

You are to be a journalist from a daily evening paper, for example, the London Evening Standard, Leicester Mercury, Birmingham Evening Mail, Sheffield Star, Glasgow Evening Times.

In terms of briefing and timescale this exercise will be as real as possible.

To give you a little background: on newspapers like the Evening Standard *there are a group of reporters who are equivalent to foot soldiers. They are non-specialist, and probably write 3–5 stories every day on any subject that the news editor decides. You are to be one of these.*

A normal day for these people will start around 7.00 a.m., as the first editions go to press by 10.30 or 11.00 a.m., and stories have to be gathered, written and edited.

So it's now about 7.30 a.m. in the newsroom and the news editor gives you your briefing:

'Some Nobel prize-winning Professor called Konrad von Klaus is arriving at Heathrow, at 10.00 a.m. He's giving a 10-minute Press Conference in the VIP Lounge – be there and I want 200 words for page 7. He's been reported in De Stern *(the German magazine) as having said that "the British are a nation of animal-loving hypocrites".'*

(This last paragraph is the kind of briefing a journalist would receive in the real world.)

At this point it would be a good idea to check that the 'students' know what it is you are asking them to do, and that they are clear about their role.

So, to move on:

'Now here we are in the VIP Lounge at Heathrow – a flunky will offer you drinks (which you'll refuse except perhaps for a cup of coffee) and when the appropriate time comes he will usher in the Professor and say "Ladies and gentlemen of the Press, may I introduce Professor Konrad von Klaus. He will give you 10 minutes of his valuable time – this is the only interview he'll be giving whilst he is visiting the UK".'

At this point one of your tutors has to play the part of the Professor and the questioning from the 'students' begins. To a greater or lesser extent (see 'The Professor's Story' below) your mock Professor has to play it on the hoof as to how he answers the questions. The press conference must stop after 10 minutes and then you give them 20–30 minutes to write their 200-word news story.

THE PROFESSOR'S STORY

Some notes for whoever is to play Professor von Klaus.

(In responding to the students questions be accurate, but not too helpful; try not to give any information that you haven't been asked for.)

- The Professor's basic story is that he's an oncology (cancer) researcher from Zurich (Switzerland) and all his research animals (24 beagles) have been 'liberated' by animal rights terrorists.
- The Professor is investigating a new compound (ZX/173/B) which he has formulated as a tumour regressor in lung cancer.
- The Professor was surgically implanting cancerous cells into the lungs of dogs, treating half the sample with the drug and using the other half as his control.
- The Professor is very angry because previous trials on small mammals (mice and rats) had a near 90% success rate (88.8%) and early signs with the dogs were very hopeful. But now because his dogs have gone, his research has been put back at least two years, and he's got to go back and start again.
- The Professor is in the UK to attend an Oncology Society Conference in York, where he was to give a paper on his latest research findings. He admits to the quote about 'the British . . .' and justifies it on the following grounds.

  First, the night-watchman, who was badly beaten up, says the leader of the terrorists 'spoke English with an English accent'.

  Second, the Home Office each year produces statistics which show that after every Christmas over 30,000 pets that have been bought as presents are thrown out on the streets and that each summer when people go on holiday, over 50,000 pets are dumped so that their owners don't have to find someone else to look after them.
- The Professor, aged 57, will give no details about the break-in at his lab (Zurich Experimental Research in Oncology Institute) or how the case is going. The police have asked him not to.
- The Professor's research is funded by the Swiss Government as well as by two pharmaceutical companies, which the Professor will not name.

- The Professor is an animal lover himself, and his family has several pets. The professor is unrepentant about his animal experimentation work. He says that tissue culture is not yet a proven means to do the work he is undertaking, but of course when it is he'll seriously consider changing to it. He also says that cancer is one of the biggest killers in the western world and he has a duty to alleviate the distress and attempt to find a cure. The professor says that in his country the attitude to animal work is sensible in that they realize the good which can arise from using animals for experimental work. In contrast, attitudes in the UK are hysterical and hypocritical.

Once the students' time is up, you need to provide feedback on their efforts. It is useful if all your tutors help in this process. Do this in two stages. First crit the 'intro', (the opening paragraph, the first one or two sentences) and then crit the rest. Pick on students at random or ask for volunteers to read out their intro. As long as your tutors are professional journalists, or at least well versed in news writing, then it is relatively easy to crit the worst offenders and to suggest, constructively, alternatives and why the alternatives are used. In such a group you often find 'gross' mistakes, for example, no one asks how the professor spells his name; what country or town he's from; how old he is; what the name of his research institute/university is; what animals he was using in his research; what the compound is called; who has financed his research; why he's in the UK and so on.

Added to these types of informational mistakes, other usual faults are: trying to tell the story chronologically; not seeing the main news point; using inappropriate language (e.g. 'oncology' rather than 'cancer', 'research subjects' rather than 'dogs'); writing in the passive voice; not having any quotes; inventing facts that haven't arisen from the interview; inserting opinion.

At the end of this session various points should have emerged:

- accurate news writing is based purely on factual information, that is, it is a straight report of what happened;
- the intro is vital as it draws the reader into the piece. The intro must answer the '5 Ws' – Who?; What?; Why?; When?; Where?; – while the remainder of the news story amplifies and explains and addresses the question 'How?'
- deadlines have to be met;
- stories have to be written to exact length;
- news journalists never write their own headlines;

- the rest of the paper will use the news piece as source information; that is the editorial writers may want to slam the professor – 'Who the hell is this man to tell us we are hypocrites?'; or the features department may want to write a longer piece on 'the state of cancer research in the UK'.

It can be useful, although not vital to finish this session by reading out a model answer – what the news story should have looked like if the 'right' questions had been asked. The model could look something like this:

WHO?   Swiss cancer specialist, Professor Konrad von Klaus, in London
WHERE? today, accused the British press of being 'a nation of animal loving
WHEN? hypocrites'. The Professor, who is researching into lung cancer,
WHAT? made the accusation after 24 beagles were 'liberated' from his clinic
WHY?   by, he said, 'English-speaking animal rights terrorists'.

Professor von Klaus is in Britain to attend a cancer conference where he was due to talk about the results of his research. 'My research, which aims to save thousands of lives has been put back at least two years by these terrorists', said the Professor.

He backed up his accusation of hypocrisy by saying that every year in Britain, according to Home Office figures, over 80,000 pets are abandoned by owners who can't be bothered with them.

The Professor's research involved 24 beagles, only half of which were treated with a new compound (ZX/173/B), after having cancer cells implanted.

The Professor was cautious about whether his treatment was a cure for cancer. He said: 'In our work on mice and rats we had an over 80% success rate but with my beagles gone I've got to go back and start all over again'.

(*192 words*)

3. Snapshots of the Media

For scientists to be able to work with the media, they first need to know how the media operates. The aim of this session, therefore, is to explain (briefly) the structure and organization of the media, where news and stories come from, who decides on what gets written, what the best ways are to access the media.

From the programme you'll see that the session is divided into three – newspapers, radio and magazines – and if you've chosen your tutors carefully, then really all you have to do is give them the aims above, tell them they've got no more than 10–15 minutes each, and sit back and listen.

If you are doing the whole of this session yourself, then a good deal of preparation is necessary, and you should find *Chapters 2, 3 and 4* of this book invaluable.

This session always throws up numerous questions, so allow a reasonable amount of time, and remember that the object of the exercise is to provide your participants with basic information about systems and organizations with which they will be very unfamiliar.

4. Media Releases

Media releases are probably the commonest and easiest means of communication with the media machine. This session, therefore, aims to tell the students why we use them, and how to produce a usable release (*NB: usable in this context means of use to the journalist*). This session should also be seen as an introduction to Session 5 which will be an exercise in actually writing a media release.

What follows here are a series of lecture notes. To fill in the detail you will find it useful to refer to *Chapter 6*.

Media Releases – why we use them

First assume that your students are past the initial hurdle of wanting to communicate with a wider audience via the media.

We use releases for three good reasons:

1) they are an accepted method for the media to receive 'stories';
2) they are efficient in that one piece of paper can be distributed to many targets;
3) they force the writer to distil and make accessible what can be complex and lengthy base information.

The ultimate object of media release production is to produce a set of words which can be used 'as is' by the target audience. The ultimate accolade is to see your release just about word for word in print.

So how can we produce the perfect release? What are the key considerations? There are four golden rules:

1) appropriate design
2) perfect timing
3) proper distribution and
4) correct composition

Design

A release is a functional document and therefore how it looks and the elements it contains are vital to the communication process. A useable/functional release should look like that in *Figure A*.

JANET: BPS_X@UK.AC.LE
Compuserve: 100020,73
Telephone: 0533 549568
Fax: 0533 470787

St. Andrews House
48, Princess Road East
LEICESTER
LE1 7DR

Masthead

The British Psychological Society

Incorporated by Royal Charter - Registered Charity No. 229642

MEDIA RELEASE

Dateline
Embargo

Date: Monday 6 April 1992
Embargo: 14.00 hrs Saturday 11 April 1992

Heading

PROBLEMS IN ASSESSING AND TREATING SPECIAL HOSPITAL PATIENTS

Text

How do you decide if someone who has committed a violent crime should be sent for treatment or sent to prison? This is one of the difficult questions raised in a symposium presented by members of Broadmoor Hospital's Psychology Department at The British Psychological Society's Annual Conference in the Spa Complex, Scarborough, today, Saturday 11 April 1992.

The symposium convened by Carol Sellars, a Chartered Clinical Psychologist, discusses the question of 'treatability' in those diagnosed as 'psychopaths', under the Mental Health Act (1983). This Act changed the law so that in order for an offender to be admitted to a Special Hospital like Broadmoor, psychiatrists and psychologists have to say that he or she will be treatable. Carol Sellars argues that this is almost impossible to do, given our present state of knowledge, and actually stops some people getting the care they need.

Other papers in the symposium include one by Dr Mary Hall, who looks at the evidence for brain damage in some of Broadmoor's patients and tries to relate this to offending.

Dr Derek Perkins talks about the problems of assessing and treating sex offenders, while Lona Roberts explains the role of the Mental Health Act Tribunals in deciding when and how Special Hospital patients should be released.

For Further
Information

FOR FURTHER INFORMATION CONTACT: Sue Cavill, Press Officer, Tel. 0533 549568 (work), 0533 000000 (home) Stephen White, Director of Information, Tel. 0533 549568 (work) 0533 000000 (home).

ON WEDNESDAY 8 APRIL ONLY CONTACT Sue Cavill or Stephen White at the Cornelian Suite, Hotel St Nicholas, Scarborough. Tel. 0723 364101.

DURING THE CONFERENCE telephone 0723 377616 or 377618. Fax 0723 377667.

Figure A. Sample media release.

Why should a release look like this? What are the vital elements?

Masthead: the recipient has to know where the release comes from. In the example shown the masthead is simply a copy of The British Psychological Society's letterhead with the addition of the words 'Media Release'. Believe it or not many releases are received without these vital words and therefore the journalist can only guess at the function of the piece of paper.

Individual journalists can and do receive hundreds of releases each day and very few are read in part and even fewer in full. So the masthead has an important function.

If the journalist has got a good story from you in the past then the sight of your masthead will ensure that the journalist stops at least long enough to read the first paragraph.

Dateline: the date here is the date sent out. This simply provides the journalist with a checking mechanism to know that the release current.

Embargo: the date and time here tells the journalist that the story cannot be used before the day and time stated. This device is of advantage to both you and the media. It allows you to release information well in advance, it allows the journalist time to consider whether or not to use it, and time to get other or contrary comment/opinion, and it means that your story should appear across the whole of the media all at the same time.

Heading: don't attempt to write clever Guardianesque headlines (very few of us have the skill); simply write a factual informative few words which tell the recipient the nub of the story.

Text: one and a half or double line space with a decent left margin. This is done so that notes and sub-editing can be efficiently handled on the page.

For further information: again this is important base information. You must give the journalists a specific contact point, name, home and work telephone numbers (journalists tend to work 'non-office' hours so early evening and Sunday mornings are not unusual times to receive calls).

No matter how perfect your release, it is unlikely that a journalist will use it without first checking a fact or two with you.

Timing

A release must reach its target in time for something to be done with it. News happens today and tomorrow, not yesterday. So we must learn what time lag is necessary between issue and potential use. This will vary according to the type of media targeted – radio can react within hours; TV longer, as they need visuals. Newspapers need at least a day and some magazines work to deadlines up to three months in advance. So an understanding of deadlines is vital.

An example is perhaps the easiest way to describe timing. For the Annual Conference of The British Psychological Society, the target journalists (specialist correspondents and features editors on the national newspapers, TV and radio, appropriate magazines, news agencies and the local media) are sent, 10–14 working days before the event, a set of releases on selected conference papers, the abstracts of all the papers and the full Conference Programme. This allows the journalists to sift and sort the information, select what stories they want to write, contact the individual paper-givers for more information and/or quotes, and to contact those with contrary viewpoints.

The same set of releases are then sent to news editors within the national media, about three or four days before the event. The object of this exercise is to hit a different audience and to ensure that the news desk is aware of the potential of the stories sent earlier to the specialists.

Distribution

Good distribution actually means a lot of waste, in that we have to think of all the people who could possibly use the story. The tradition within science is simply to target the science correspondent and the specialist science magazine. But rather than this 'knee-jerk' reaction we need to look at the content of each individual story before we decide who to send it to.

Trying to give examples here is not that easy, but two or three might help to illustrate the point: a paper describing a new lightweight metal which withstood high temperatures might well also be targeted at the motoring and/or aviation correspondent; a paper describing the discovery of the effect of a chemical toxin found in some foods should also go to the medical and/or health correspondent; a paper highlighting some new ergonomic advance should also go to the industrial specialist.

So who should receive our releases? At the local geographical level then, the answer is fairly simple as you should know who the local media are – newspapers daily and weekly, radio, TV, press agencies, freelances plus any appropriate locally based magazines. If you move onto the national level, then developing a distribution list can be a very time consuming, but necessary, exercise, as the options are so great. (One of the best purchases you can make – or try your local library first – is to get hold of a good directory which lists all the possible media, suitably categorized. A good one to look at is *Editors* published by PR Newslink. It is in six volumes, regularly updated and contains the names of specialist correspondents as well as a publication profile.)

Composition

This does not relate just to the words we use, but also the style. As was said, the perfect release aims to ape a newspaper news story. So one of the best ways of learning the tricks of the trade is to actually read newspapers, and to read them in a way which analyses their style, content and structure.

The most common faults of non-news writers and especially scientists are:

- use of jargon and long words;
- overly complex sentence construction;
- being chronological;
- bad article structure (either leaving the results till last or even not giving the results at all).

So, if we can recognize the faults, then what are the golden rules to ensure we write a correct and usable release?

Be active. We must use the active voice in our writing rather than the passive voice, for example:

Jones was arrested by the police – PASSIVE;
Police arrested Jones – ACTIVE (and shorter).

A meeting will be held by the committee next week – PASSIVE;
The committee meets next week – ACTIVE (and shorter).

The simple rule to remember is:

SUBJECT – VERB – OBJECT

Be positive. In other words delete all the negatives from our writing – tell the reader what happened rather than what didn't happen, for example:

The experiments were not successful – NEGATIVE;
The experiments failed – POSITIVE (and shorter).

The MRC say they will not now proceed with their plans – NEGATIVE;
The MRC say they have dropped their plans – POSITIVE (and shorter).

The Ethics Committee did not pay attention to the complaint – NEGATIVE;
The ethics committee ignored the complaint – POSITIVE (and shorter).

Be concise. This little rule covers two linked faults which need
remedying. First, science's natural mode of writing sentences
which are too long, and second, science's tendency to write sentences which are too complicated. The rule to remember is – only
one idea per sentence.
   To combat this fault we need to understand the three basic types
of sentence construction: the *simple*; the *compound*; and the *complex*.

The simple sentence has one subject and one statement:

Eight people joined the branch yesterday.

The compound sentence is two simple sentences joined together
(usually with the word 'and'):

*Eight people joined the branch yesterday and brought the total membership
to 1013.*

The complex sentence has one main statement, but one (or more)
subordinate and qualifying clauses:

*Eight people, from the Education Department, joined the branch yesterday
as a result of the current recruitment campaign, bringing the total
membership to 1013.*

If you read newspapers, you'll find that there is a preponderance
of 'simple' and 'compound' sentences and relatively few 'complex'
sentences (even in the quality press). This is very deliberate. Newspapers know, via market research, what their readers can comprehend easily, and too many complex sentences, in any one article,
are a barrier to understanding. To ape their style therefore, our
releases must be structurally correct.
   Words too will have been analysed by the press in terms of
whether their readers will understand them. All the words in the
first column in *Table A* are banned because their meaning is

unclear. (They have all been taken from newspaper style books –
the books provided to all newspaper journalists which list the
'house rules'.) The alternatives, which are shorter, clearer and
unambiguous are listed in the second column.

Table A 'Banned' words and their alternatives
'Don't use big words where shorter ones will do.'

TRY TO AVOID:	USE INSTEAD:
accordingly	so
apparent	clear, plain
commence	start, begin
consult	talk to, see, meet
discontinue, terminate	stop, end
dwelling, residence,	home
economical	cheap
endeavour, attempt	try
erroneous	wrong, false
facilitate	help
in consequence of	because
in excess of	more than
initiate	start
necessitate	need, require
obtain, receive	get
regulation	rule
state	say
statutory	legal, by law
supplementary	extra, more
utilize	use

So, to sum up:
- Be active.
- Be positive.
- Be concise.
- Avoid jargon (and cliches).
- Write for your audience (the journalists and the public beyond –
  not your peers).
- Always use first names with surnames, not just initials.
- Be accurate (always check your facts).
- Grab your readers' attention – the intro is vital. This last point

should be heavily reinforced. The first sentence must contain the nub, the news. Even if all the rest is wrong this has to be got right.

Finally, remember you've only got one side of A4 to put your message over (200–250 words), so every word and every sentence matters.

5. Media Release Writing Exercise

The object of this session is very simple – to see if the students have learnt anything from the previous session.

Try to make the exercise as real as possible by providing them with base information with which they are familiar, at least in terms of general content. I find abstracts/summaries of conference papers the best source material.

Give out the abstracts/summaries to each individual participant. (If you've got about 16 students and three or four tutors then use three or four different abstracts – this means that each tutor will only have four or five media release to crit.)

Tell the students they have 30–40 minutes to produce a 200-word release on the abstract provided. They are to work alone and to produce the finished product so that it can be read by someone else and it must have their name on it (one would hate to criticize the wrong person!).

Some people will find this exercise very difficult. Try to check every 10 minutes or so. If it looks like a coronary is setting in, then amend the brief so that they at least produce the first two or three paragraphs.

At the end of this session you should have a media release from each individual, with their name on it. These can be given to the tutors for them to crit whilst Session 6 is in progress.

6. Being Interviewed

Over and above the press release, the main way journalists get their information is by interviewing the person who has done the work. Unless you understand the interview technique this process can be very daunting.

Hopefully you'll get your 'radio' tutor to give this session. This has the advantage of allowing you to cover not just the print journalist's telephone enquiry, but also the different types of interview scenario which could be encountered in the electronic media.

The hints and tips in *Appendix 2* should be covered, either by lecture, discussion or role play.

7. Media Releases Review

This session should provide your students with positive and constructive feed-back on the releases they wrote in Session 5.

You can either do the crit. as a plenary or divide the students up into the three or four groups depending on which release they wrote. (Three or four small groups can work easily in one room.) Then simply let your tutors loose.

8. Final Round-Up and Close

By this time both your participants and your tutors will be tired and suffering from information overload. However, a final few minutes to try and pull together the main lessons of the day, and to allow the students to raise any major outstanding questions, is always a good way to finish off.

The final send-off should include an offer by you to help any of the students with any media communications problems they may encounter in the future.

Being Interviewed – Hints and Tips

The interview by a professional from the media can be a nerve-racking experience. However, there are some simple hints, tips and rules which should make your performance better and therefore make the media happy that they've got a good piece of tape or print.

The basic guidelines are:

- **know the basis of the interview;**
- **know the questions;**
- **know your subject.**

Although the general hints are the same for all parts of the media, there are some minor differences. For ease of explanation I will deal with TV, radio and newspapers separately.

Television

TV interviews come in three types – the live studio interview, the filmed studio interview, the location (usually your place of work) interview.

What to do beforehand

First, find out the purpose of the interview, in other words, why you are there. This may sound obvious but there are many examples of interviewees being completely thrown by the questions because they hadn't checked on the ground rules. So, find out the purpose and find out at least the first question that you will be asked – more if possible, but the first will give you a chance to prepare a brief and direct response. It also gives you an opportunity to negotiate the first question if you think it is inappropriate or unhelpful.

Other things you should find out about:

- Is it live or recorded, and if it's recorded will the tape be edited?

If it is to be edited this gives you the chance to stop the interview, apologize and ask to give your answer again.

- How are you going to be introduced? Saves them getting your name, title and place of work wrong.
- How long is the interview to last – three questions, six or ten questions? This will give you a good guide as to whether you must be succinct or whether you can be slightly more leisurely.
- Are you to be interviewed alone or is there another guest? If there is someone else, get a good breakdown of their position so that you know if the interview is going to be mutually supportive or confrontational.

Also, get to the studio at least an hour in advance. This gives you the chance to calm down, have a coffee, check with the producer/interviewer about questions and gives you the chance to become familiar with the studio – a rather daunting place full of lights, cameras, microphones, monitors and lots of people.

During the interview

If you have followed the pre-interview rules, than the event itself should be painless. However, a few tips may help your performance.

- Many novice interviewees attempt to pack their answers with a welter of information – don't. Try to work out in advance the 3 or 4 most important points you wish to get across and say them in the simplest way you can. It really doesn't matter whether you directly answer the question, the object of the exercise is to get your points over.
- Your language is vital. Your audience will not understand technical terminology – so find simple alternatives for your normal jargon.
- Although your audience could be several million, the best interviews are those where interviewer and interviewee are in conversation. So don't declaim, patronize, or lecture and don't look straight at the camera – your eye contact should be with the interviewer. (The only time when you have to look at the camera is when you are being interviewed in a remote studio, with your interviewer perhaps hundreds of miles away.)
- Try to dress quietly. Busy cloth patterns are accentuated by TV and your audience may remember your checked shirt, striped tie or floral blouse rather than what you said.

- Tinted spectacles on screen will make you look like the Mafia.
- Don't take notes into the studio – you will be forever looking down or sideways to check if you have made all your points. If you have only got three points to make you should be able to remember them.
- Try not to jump about, or wave your arms; even a relatively small movement can mean you disappear out of shot.
- Finally, if you have a speech impediment or just freeze at the prospect of cameras and lights then get a colleague to do the interview.

Radio

What has been said about television goes for radio too except that the pressure of being seen is removed. So your clothing doesn't matter, neither do your gesticulations, but remember that whereas a gesture can be worth a thousand words on TV you can't use a gesture on radio. You can also take some simple notes into a studio with you. In fact for the phone-in, a pad and pen is essential. (First write down the caller's name and then the pertinent point(s) of their question.)

Radio interviews can also be done down a phone-line. If possible avoid this path as the sound quality is never perfect. Always try and get to the studio, or get the reporter to come to you to tape the interview face-to-face.

The Press

The printed media comes in so many different forms that you could almost do with separate chapters on each; however space does not permit elongated explanations.

Journalists, and especially those on newspapers, may not know anything about your subject but they are very skilled at asking pertinent questions and extracting information.

The printed press sometimes has 'an angle' – an editorial point they wish to make. So, when approached always ask what the angle is and if you don't like it, either attempt a re-negotiation or simply say 'no thanks'.

Print journalists tend to collect their stories and comments over the phone, and it is very easy to be more forthcoming than intended down a phone line.

Two tips may help:

- pretend that your professional colleagues are in the room with you;
- don't answer the questions on the spot. Ask the journalist to give you all the questions, then put the phone down and call back in 10/15/30 minutes. If you use this technique you must phone back.

This technique also gives you the chance to sort your thoughts, work out the most important points, and write down a few direct quotes.

Of course there will always be subsidiary questions and points of clarification but if you have done your homework these shouldn't prove either difficult or embarrassing.

A final point which you may find useful

'Off-the-record' is a means for you to provide information for a journalist's use but without you being quoted. There may be an occasion to use this device, and you can be 95% sure that a journalist will not break this convention.

If a journalist does, then you will never speak to them again and as journalists live by their sources this is a serious repercussion.

Remember to always say 'this is off-the-record' before you say something. There is nothing more frustrating to a journalist than to have taken copious notes and then to be told 'by the way, that is off-the-record'.

Remember, being interviewed by a journalist in either TV, radio or the press should not be a harrowing experience as long as you have followed the rules:

- **know the basis of the interview;**
- **know the questions;**
- **know your subject.**

Reproduced by kind permission of the Press Committee, The British Psychological Society.

Appendix 3

Useful Publications

Editors, published by PR Newslink. This is a six-volume directory which covers the whole of the UK media (Volume 6 covers the London correspondents of the foreign press). The various volumes are regularly updated – Volume 1 on the National Press, News Agencies, Radio and TV is monthly; and Volume 4, which lists all the consumer and leisure magazines, is published quarterly. *Editors'* great use is that it lists all the staff on the national papers.

Willings Press Guide, published annually by Reed Information Services. This directory lists all the titles in publication in the UK. It also lists publishers and all their titles. (Volume 2 lists various publications in the USA and other countries.) One of the best things about *Willings* is that it lists all the 'scientific' journals.

The Blue Book of British Broadcasting, published annually by Tellex Monitors. *The Blue Book* does for broadcasting what *Willings* does for print. It lists all the network companies, their programmes, and their staff.

Directory of British Film and TV Producers, published annually by PACT (**Producers'** Alliance for Cinema and Television). With more and more production going to outside companies this guide will become increasingly useful. All the companies listed are members of PACT, so there may be some notable omissions. Each company is listed with address as well as both past and current productions.

Newsman's English, Harold Evans, published by Heinemann. This is probably the best book ever written on the craft of writing for newspapers. It's full of excellent examples and shows clearly how turgid classic prose can be turned into interesting news writing. *Newsman's English* is the first of five detailed volumes in a series. The other books in the series are *Handling Newspaper Text*, *News Headlines*, *Picture Editing* and *Newspaper Design*.

Writers' & Artists' Yearbook, published annually by A & C Black. This yearbook is a comprehensive handbook for writers and is especially useful for those just starting out.

Appendix 4

Complaints

One of the great truths about dealing with the media is that journalists sometimes make mistakes; like the rest of us, they aren't perfect. At some time you may be so aggrieved that you will want to complain. So here is a quick DIY checklist of what to do and how to do it.

The first thing to say is that it helps if you have kept some kind of note of what you've actually said (or written), since memory can be very selective and inaccurate. So, to complain, the following steps should be taken (in order):

1. Phone (or write or fax) the individual journalist and explain your complaint. Ask for a correction/apology.
2. Phone (or write or fax) the news editor (or features editor if it was a feature), explain your complaint and ask for a correction/ apology.
3. Write to the editor with your complaint requesting/demanding a correction/apology (keep a copy of the letter).
   NB You may be offered the chance to write a 'Letter to the Editor' for publication in the Letters column. That may satisfy you, but it is always preferable to have a correction printed in the same section of the paper as that in which the original offending story appeared. The reason is that the readers (who read the original) are more likely to see the correction here than they are to read the Letters column, even if it is *The Times*.
4. Write to the 'Readers' Representative'. All main newspapers now have such a person whose job it is to adjudicate on complaints.
5. Use the rival newspapers/media to make your complaint a story in its own right. (As a method of complaining this may work, but you must realize that it has to be a 'big' and 'serious' issue/ news story.)
6. Complain to the Press Complaints Commission. (They are very helpful and will explain how to make your complaint.)
7. Complain to the journalists' union, the National Union of Journalists. Under their *Code of Conduct* and rules it is possible to

file a specific complaint against a named journalist, although, of course, not all journalists belong to the NUJ.

Complaints and complaining are never satisfactory. By the very nature of the media, the correction, apology or 'Letter to the Editor' may not be seen by the same people who read/saw the original offending item. However, complaining is important. If we don't complain formally, then it is difficult to grumble when the same mistakes are made in the future. Complaining is an essential part of pressure for change.

NB   These points mainly apply to newspapers and to a lesser extent TV and radio. There is a formal complaints machine for the electronic media, The Broadcasting Complaints Commission.

ADDRESSES

Broadcasting Complaints Commission, 35 Grosvenor Gardens, London SW11 OBS, Telephone 071 630 1966

National Union of Journalists, 314 Grays Inn Road, London WC1X 8DP, Telephone 071 278 7916

Press Complaints Commission, 1 Salisbury Square, London EC4Y 8AE, Telephone 071 353 1248